Stitch AND Split
Appliqué

12 RAW-EDGE PROJECTS

Jayme Crow and Joan Segna

Martingale®
& COMPANY

MISSION STATEMENT

*Dedicated to providing quality products
and service to inspire creativity.*

CREDITS

President ✤ Nancy J. Martin
CEO ✤ Daniel J. Martin
Publisher ✤ Jane Hamada
Editorial Director ✤ Mary V. Green
Managing Editor ✤ Tina Cook
Technical Editor ✤ Laurie Baker
Copy Editor ✤ Mary Martin
Design Director ✤ Stan Green
Illustrator ✤ Laurel Strand
Cover Designer ✤ Stan Green
Text Designer ✤ Regina Girard
Photographer ✤ Brent Kane

Stitch and Split Appliqué: 12 Raw-Edge Projects
© 2004 Jayme Crow and Joan Segna

That Patchwork Place® is an imprint
of Martingale & Company®.

Martingale & Company
20205 144th Avenue NE
Woodinville, WA 98072-8478 USA
www.martingale-pub.com

Printed in China
09 08 07 06 05 04   8 7 6 5 4 3 2 1

Library of Congress Cataloging-in-Publication Data
Crow, Jayme.
    Stitch and split appliqué : 12 raw-edge projects /
Jayme Crow and Joan Segna.
        p. cm.
    ISBN 1-56477-528-3
    1. Appliqué—Patterns. I. Segna, Joan. II. Title.
    TT779 .S37 2004
    746.46'041—dc22
                                                            2003027007

Dedication

This book and thoughts of family are dedicated to Carol Hope, my sister and friend. All of the stitches she so carefully sewed have given her family the strength to go on.

Joan

Acknowledgments

We owe our heartfelt thanks to our support crew:

Sandy "magic fingers" Sims of Heirloom Originals—the machine quilter extraordinaire. You will see her beautiful handiwork throughout this book.

Jerrine "I can't believe you guys" Kirsch—who tests and teaches our patterns. Her expertise is invaluable, and her enthusiasm is contagious.

Megan "let's try this" Cook—budding designer. Her creative ideas are often used to enhance our designs.

Kristi "can do" Wenrich—we wish we could clone her.

Beverly "got a new machine" Hobbs—so she used it!

Sandra "up for a challenge" Blake—she tried a new quilting technique when testing our patterns.

Louann "I am only a beginner" Krass—but not for long!

Liz "upstairs" Nieman—Liz lived above the studio for one year. Liz, come back!

George "upstairs" Nieman—he lived with Liz. He tried to keep us tidy!

Penny "wow" Colton—our "picture-perfect" cheerleader.

Sheila "wordsmith" Bennett—she crossed our *t*'s and dotted our *i*'s.

Don "bright idea" Segna—we actually do use his ideas once in a while.

Jim "gofer" Crow—need we say more? Jim does it all.

Our appreciation goes to the Martingale family, for without them there would be no book!

And a special thanks to all the companies whose products we used in our quilts: Andover Fabrics; Bold Over Batiks!; Gütermann; American & Efird Inc.; YLI Corporation; Things Japanese; The Warm Company; Beacon Adhesives Co. Inc.; and Artemis Exquisite Embellishments.

CONTENTS

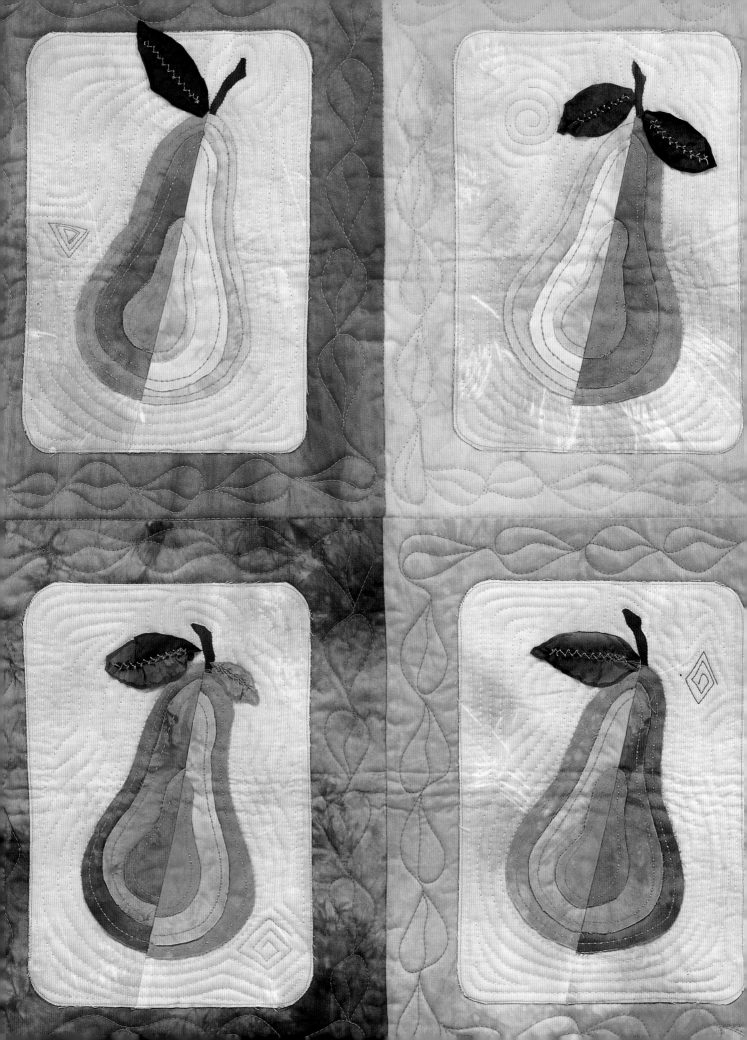

*B*ella *nonna* is Italian and means beautiful grandmother. Every woman who has held a needle and thread has probably had a special grandmother, mother, or aunt who lovingly guided her through her first sewing project. We chose the name *Bella Nonna* for our company to honor the sewing traditions of our "beautiful grandmothers" and keep them close to us.

This book is a collaboration between two women who love to work with fabric, color, and design. Our design studio is tucked away on a half acre in Kennewick, Washington, and feels a bit like Grandmother's house with its floral carpet, lace curtains, and a pot of coffee brewing on the counter. But more than coffee brews here. (Hold on to your hat, Granny!) We've got lots of fun ideas to share, and this book is all about one of them—split designs.

Simply stated, split-design quilts are made by cutting out several sizes of the same shape from different fabrics. The shapes are layered into units from largest to smallest and stitched together using a raw-edge appliqué technique. Several units are made from different fabrics. Next each unit is cut into halves, thirds, or even quarters. Then pieces from different units are stitched back together to create the original shape. The entire process is explained in depth in "The Split-Design Process," beginning on page 11.

Our grandmothers would never have left raw edges exposed on their quilts, but for us it is liberating to realize that all edges don't have to be securely tucked under. Because of this, we can now achieve forms that once were thought impossible in the geometric world of quilting. Even though we try to make edges match and sew with the straightest of seams, the one thing we cannot compromise is our creativity. And because the quilting world has been more receptive to new ideas in the past 20 years, creativity can come first—without the old constraints of always having to match colors, points, and seams.

Along with this new liberation, quilters have a kaleidoscope of fabric colors and textures available, new products to expand their repertoire of techniques, and a willingness to be more playful in selecting and combining the color palette. (And yes, Granny, you can use lots of different reds together and your project will look great!)

We invite you to shed your old constraints and start stepping out with new colors, patterns, and textures—and, of course, a raw edge or two!

FABRIC SELECTION

As the saying goes, "The soup is only as good as the ingredients." Your quilt will be only as good as the fabrics you choose. Purchase top-quality 100%-cotton fabrics for the best results. We recommend prewashing your fabrics to remove any excess dyes that may bleed onto other quilt fabrics and to ensure that your finished quilt will shrink evenly when washed. The yardage amounts listed under "Materials" for each project assume 42" of useable fabric after prewashing.

These projects provide lots of opportunity for digging into your fabric stash or buying fat quarters, because split-design quilts use lots of different fabrics to give them their unique look. For example, "Park Bench Posies" on page 18 uses 24 different fabrics for the flowers. You may be thinking, "Zowie! How can I choose that many fabrics that all work together?" Well, it's not as difficult as it sounds if you just follow a few simple guidelines.

First, decide on a color family. No matter which color family you choose, our simple explanation works. Let's say you want a "Park Bench Posies" quilt full of red poppies. True red is a primary color, and every other red is a mixture of true red and one or more colors, but they are all in the red color family. The more fabrics that you use with "red blood" in them, the happier the family becomes. Look at it this way: Mr. Red-Violet and his wife, Mrs. Red-Orange, have many children. They don't all look alike, but put them together and they make a happy family!

A happy color family should also include solids, plaids, and prints. When the relatives of Mr. and Mrs. Red show up, the extended family includes solid uncles, plaid aunts, and playful cousins in many different prints. All together, they have a family reunion, and it is a beautiful sight.

Granny shows up in her fuchsia polka-dot dress, rust plaid jacket, and solid magenta hat and fits right in!

As you select your fabrics, be mindful of color values. Appliqué shapes that progress in value from dark at the outer edge to light at the center will appear to recede at the outer edge and advance at the center. In contrast, if the values progress from light at the outer edge to dark at the center, the center will appear to recede. Using all of the same color value will make your project appear flat. Let's use those red poppies in the "Park Bench Posies" quilt as an example again. In this quilt, each flower is made up of three concentric layers. If you want flowers that get darker as they go toward the center, cut all of the large flowers from a light value, all of the medium flowers from a medium value, and all of the small flowers from a dark value. Of course, for a different effect, you could reverse the color value, using a dark value for the large flowers and a light value for the small flowers. Or you could choose to vary the values within each flower, giving the flowers a whimsical, mix-and-match look when they are cut apart and resewn.

Still not convinced that all your fabric choices will work together? Try focusing on one motif at a time, in this case one flower. Each flower uses three fabrics, so choose three that you like together. Then do the same for the remaining seven flowers. If the mix of fabrics for each flower is pleasing, you'll have a happy family when you cut them apart and rearrange them.

To add punch or spark to your project, place the main color family against a complementary color family. For the "Park Bench Posies" project, a value range of green leaves does the trick. Be daring and make your colors dance!

THE SPLIT-DESIGN PROCESS

*E*ach project in this book follows the same general process for making the split-design elements within the quilt. This section contains the step-by-step details of the process as well as some tips to make a successful split-design quilt. Any variations in the process will be dealt with in the individual project instructions.

Step 1: Make the Templates

Patterns are provided with each project for making the templates required to cut the appliqué shapes. Some patterns are too large to fit on a single page. These patterns have been reduced or, when the pattern is symmetrical, given as half-patterns. If a pattern has been reduced, enlarge it to the percentage indicated using a photocopy machine, and then make the template as described below. For a half-pattern, take a piece of paper that is large enough to accommodate the full-size pattern and fold it in half vertically. Align the paper fold with the pattern's center line and trace the pattern onto the paper. Cut out the pattern on the marked line. Use the pattern to make the template as described below.

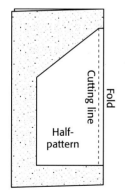

To make a template, use a sharp pencil or fine-tip marker to trace the full-size pattern onto the *dull side* of a piece of freezer paper. Transfer the cutting line(s) and any other markings to the template, as well as the name of the piece. Cut out the template on the line.

Step 2: Cut Out the Appliqué Shapes

Iron the freezer-paper template to the right side of the appropriate fabric, *shiny side down*. Cut close to the edges of the template to cut out the appliqué shape. Remove the template from the appliqué. Reuse the template as many times as necessary to cut the required fabric pieces.

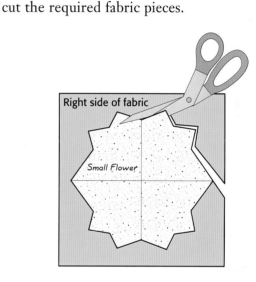

Step 3: Press the Appliqué Shapes

Press each appliqué shape, applying spray starch for stability while sewing. If you did not prewash your fabric, applying spray starch may not be necessary. Using the pattern as a guide, fold the appliqués right sides together along the cutting lines and lightly press the fold. The fold line will be used for centering the shapes and cutting the layered units apart.

Step 4: Arrange the Appliqué Units

Select the shapes needed for each appliqué unit. For example, in "Park Bench Posies," each unit is made up of one small, one medium, and one large flower shape. Layer the shapes from largest to smallest, using the fold lines as a guide for centering the shapes on each other. Lay out all of the layered units. A design board or other large surface is helpful for this task. Be sure that each unit is different and that none of the units has two shapes cut from the same fabric. Rearrange the pieces as necessary until you are pleased with the mix. If each group has a pleasing mixture of light, medium, and dark prints at this stage, then you will be pleased with the results when they are cut apart and arranged into new units.

Step 5: Raw-Edge Appliqué

The appliqué shapes are stitched together in the order they were layered in step 4, beginning with the largest shape and working toward the smallest. Depending on the project, the largest shape may or may not be stitched to a background piece before the units are cut apart. For example, in "Park Bench Posies" the largest flower is stitched to the background first, the medium flower is stitched to the large flower, and then the small flower is stitched to the medium flower. In contrast, the sunflower shapes in "Field of Sunflowers" are stitched to each other, cut apart, stitched back together, and then stitched to the background.

Let's use "Park Bench Posies" to demonstrate the technique. The process is the same for quilts in which the appliqués are stitched together first and then applied to the background, except that you stitch the pieces to the background last rather than first.

1. Center the large flower on the right side of a background square. Set your machine for a straight stitch; a narrow, open zigzag stitch; or a decorative stitch. Stitch around the shape ¼" from the raw edge; backstitch.

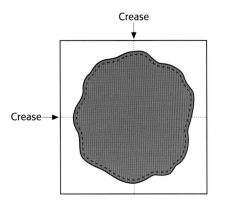

Note: If you prefer not to leave the raw edges exposed, you may hand or machine appliqué the pieces in place using your favorite appliqué method.

2. Turn the square to the wrong side and cut away the background fabric behind the large flower, leaving a ¼" seam allowance. It helps to pinch the background fabric together behind the appliqué shape and make a small slit to begin. Be careful not to cut through the top layer.

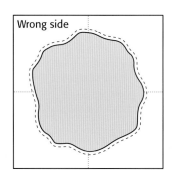

3. Turn the square to the right side and center the medium flower over the large flower. Stitch ¼" from the edges. Turn the square to the wrong side and cut out the large flower fabric from behind the medium flower, leaving a ¼" seam allowance.

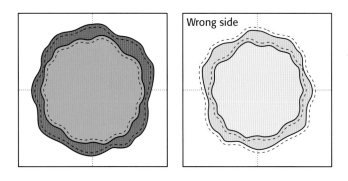

4. Continue stitching the appliqué shapes to the background in the same manner, cutting away the fabric from behind the appliqué before adding the next shape.

5. Press the blocks or appliquéd shapes from the wrong side.

Step 6: Cut Apart and Rearrange the Units

Once the units are appliquéd, use a ruler and rotary cutter to cut them into halves, thirds, or quarters, depending on the pattern. Make sure you cut the pieces apart on the fold lines that you pressed into each shape in Step 3.

Arrange pieces from different units together to form the original shape. Always rearrange all of the units and lay them out according to the quilt assembly diagram before stitching the pieces together. This will prevent you from repeating pieces within a group and will ensure that you are happy with the arrangement. Stitch the pieces together. Usually the pieces will not match at the seams, but that is part of the charm of split designs! Press the seams open.

Square up the blocks to the size indicated in the project instructions. Because distortion often occurs during the process, block backgrounds are cut 1" larger than needed and trimmed to the required size after the appliqués are stitched in place.

Step 7: Assembling the Quilt Top

Appliqué units that were not stitched to a background before they were cut apart will now be stitched to the background. In some cases, such as "Dancing Stars" (page 91), the units are stitched to blocks that are then stitched into rows. In other cases, such as "Field of Sunflowers" (page 30), the background is one piece.

When sewing rows together, press the block seams in alternate directions from row to row. This reduces bulk and makes it easier to match seams.

Step 8: Add the Borders

The materials section for each project will indicate the width and number of strips to cut from the border fabric(s). Cut the strips across the fabric width, from selvage to selvage. The strips will be trimmed to the required length or pieced to make strips long enough to border the quilt.

To add borders to your quilt, follow these steps:

1. Measure through the center of the quilt from top to bottom. Cut two border strips to this measurement. If the length is longer than 42", stitch two strips together using a bias seam (refer to "Binding" on page 15) and trim the strip to the measured length. Mark the center edges of both the quilt sides and the border strips. Stitch the strips to the sides of the quilt top, matching the centers and ends. Press the seams toward the borders.

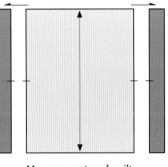

Measure center of quilt,
top to bottom. Mark centers.

2. Measure the width of the quilt from side to side, including the border strips just added. Cut two border strips to this measurement, piecing as necessary. Mark the center of the quilt's top and bottom edges and the border strips. Stitch the strips to the top and bottom edges of the quilt top, matching centers and ends. Press the seams toward the borders.

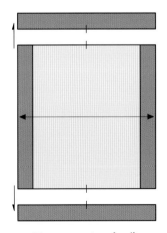

Measure center of quilt,
side to side, including borders.
Mark centers.

FINISHING YOUR QUILT

*I*t's a great feeling to complete your quilt top, but your quilt isn't finished until it's quilted and bound. This section provides the basics for completing your project so it can be enjoyed and appreciated for generations to come.

Marking the Quilting Design

If you plan to use a quilting design to enhance the pattern, mark it on the quilt top before you layer the quilt. Test the marking tool on a scrap of the quilt fabric before you mark the top to make sure the marks can be easily removed. If you are planning to quilt in the ditch, follow the outline of a motif, or free-motion quilt, there is no need to mark the design.

Layering and Basting

Cut your backing and batting pieces 3" to 4" bigger than the quilt top on all sides. For some quilts, it may be necessary to piece two or three lengths of backing fabric together to make a piece the required size. If piecing is required, trim away the selvages before stitching. Press the seams open to make quilting easier. Take the batting out of the package and let it relax before you assemble the quilt layers.

To assemble the layers, lay the backing, wrong side up, on a flat surface, such as a tabletop or floor. Smooth out the wrinkles and secure the edges with masking tape or binder clips, making sure the fabric is taut but not stretched. Place the batting over the backing and smooth out any wrinkles, working from the center out. Center the pressed top over the batting, right side up. Smooth out any wrinkles. If you are machine quilting, use rustproof safety pins to pin the layers together. Place the pins approximately 4" to 6" apart. If you are hand quilting, thread-baste the layers together, beginning at the center and working out.

Quilting

We've all heard the saying "quilting makes the quilt." It certainly can enhance your design and add dimension, no matter whether you are quilting by hand or machine. We have added quilting suggestions to each project, but it is truly your own choice.

No matter which quilting method you use, it is important to begin by stabilizing the layers. This can be done by quilting along the block edges or stitching in the ditch of each seam. Begin in the center of the quilt and work out. If you are machine quilting, a walking foot is invaluable for feeding the layers evenly through the machine.

Binding

Consider the binding as the outermost portion of the frame you create around your quilt. Audition fabrics for the binding just as you would for the borders.

The cutting instructions for each project give the number of 2¼"-wide strips to cut. Cut the strips across the width of the fabric. If you use a lofty batting, consider cutting your strips 2½" wide. You will need enough strips to go around the perimeter of the quilt plus 10" for corners and joining. Using a bias seam, stitch the strips together to create one long strip. To sew a bias seam, cross the ends of two strips right sides together at right angles. Use a sharp pencil or fabric marker to draw a diagonal line across the strips as shown. Then stitch on the marked line. Trim the seam allowance to ¼" and press the seam open.

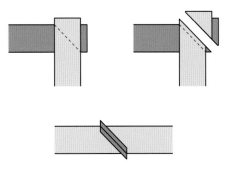

To stitch the binding to the quilt edges, follow these steps:

1. Trim one end of the binding strip at a 45° angle. Press the angled end under ¼". Press the binding strip in half, wrong sides together.

2. Trim the backing and batting even with the quilt top.

3. Open the angled end of the binding and place the binding on the quilt top right side, several inches from a corner. Align the binding and quilt raw edges. Stitch through one binding thickness for about 3", using a ¼"-wide seam allowance; backstitch and cut the threads. Refold the binding so it is doubled. Continue stitching where you left off, stitching through both binding thicknesses. End stitching ¼" from the corner of the quilt and backstitch. Clip the threads.

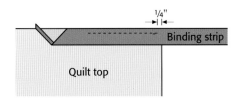

4. Turn the quilt so you will be ready to sew down the next side. Fold the binding strip up at a 45° angle and then back down on itself, with raw edges aligned. Begin stitching ¼" from the corner, backstitching to secure the stitches. Continue sewing the binding to the quilt, ending the stitching ¼" from the corner; backstitch and clip the threads.

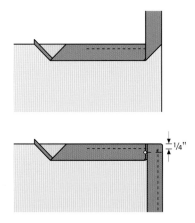

5. Repeat step 4 for the remaining corners. When you reach the beginning of the binding strip, stop stitching and leave the needle in the binding. Trim the end of the binding so it is just long enough to tuck inside the pocket formed by the single thickness. Tuck the end of the binding into the pocket and continue stitching through all thicknesses; backstitch.

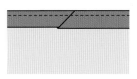

6. Fold the binding to the back of the quilt and hand stitch it in place.

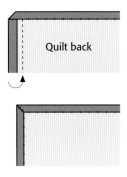

Adding a Hanging Sleeve

Quilts that will be used as wall hangings should have a sleeve tacked to the back to hold a hanging rod. Make sleeves a generous width to accommodate all rod diameters. Make the sleeve from a piece of fabric 6" to 8" wide and 1" to 2" shorter than the finished width of the quilt. Hem each end of the sleeve by turning under the raw edges ½" and stitching in place. Fold the strip in half lengthwise, wrong sides together, and stitch the raw edges together using a ¼" seam. Fold the tube so that the seam is centered on one side; press the seam open.

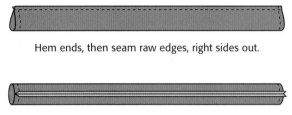

Hem ends, then seam raw edges, right sides out.

Center seam and press open.

Place the tube on the back side of the quilt just below the top binding, with the seam against the quilt. Hand sew the top edge of the sleeve to the quilt. Be careful not to stitch through the front of the quilt.

Quilt back

Tack down top edge of sleeve.

Push the front side of the tube up so the top edge covers about half the binding (this will provide a little "give" so the hanging rod does not put strain on the quilt). Sew the bottom edge of the sleeve in place as shown.

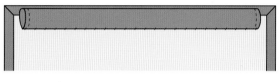

Push tube up and tack down bottom edge.

Slide a rod or dowel through the sleeve. Suspend the rod on brackets.

Labeling Your Work

It is important to add a label to your work so that future generations will have a record of who made the quilt, when it was made, and why. Labels can be as simple or elaborate as you choose, written on muslin with permanent ink or printed on fabric with the aid of your computer. Just be sure to add as much information as possible so the "story" can live on.

PARK BENCH POSIES

Finished Quilt Size: 30" x 51"
Finished Block Size: 10½"

Pieced by Jayme Crow. Machine quilted by Sandy Sims, Heirloom Originals.

I remember picking posies for my mother when I was a child. They were little weed bouquets sprinkled with Johnny-jump-ups, alfalfa blooms, dandelions, and clover. She always lovingly put them in a miniature container and placed them on the kitchen windowsill. Joan and I made our quilt using four color families—red, yellow, purple, and blue. The materials here call for these same color families, but you can use as many or as few colors as you'd like. Just be sure to vary the color values and prints when choosing fabrics.

—Jayme

Materials

Yardage is based on 42"-wide fabric.

- ❖ 1⅛ yards of white for block backgrounds
- ❖ ¾ yard of blue for border
- ❖ 1 fat quarter *each* of 3 different greens for leaves
- ❖ 1 fat quarter of blue that coordinates with border for border corner squares
- ❖ 2 squares, 11" x 11", from *each* of 4 different color families for large flowers (8 total)
- ❖ 2 squares, 10" x 10", from *each* of the same 4 color families as large flowers for medium flowers (8 total)
- ❖ 2 squares, 8" x 8", from *each* of the same 4 color families as medium and large flowers for small flowers (8 total)
- ❖ 1⅞ yards of fabric for backing
- ❖ ½ yard of fabric for binding
- ❖ 38" x 59" piece of batting
- ❖ Small bag of polyester fiberfill for stuffing leaves
- ❖ 1 bag of cream Bella Nonna petals* or 12 cream 1"- to 2"-diameter buttons for flower centers

- ❖ Freezer paper
- ❖ Spray starch
- ❖ Fabric glue

* *If you can't find Bella Nonna petals locally, ask your retailer to order them from us: Bella Nonna LLC, 608 S. Jefferson, Kennewick, WA 99336, 509-946-4859; Web site, www.bellanonnaquilt.com.*

Cutting

All measurements include ¼"-wide seam allowances.

From the white fabric, cut:
8 squares, 12" x 12"

From the border fabric, cut:
4 strips, 5" x 42"

From the border corner fabric, cut:
4 squares, 5" x 5"

From the backing fabric, cut:
1 piece, 38" x 59"

From the binding fabric, cut:
5 strips, 2¼" x 42"

Cutting the Flowers and Leaves

1. Enlarge the flower patterns on page 22 by the percentage indicated. Trace the enlarged flower patterns and the large and small leaf patterns on page 23 onto freezer paper and cut them out.

2. Use the large flower template to cut one shape from each of the eight large-flower fabrics. Repeat with the medium and small flower templates and the appropriate fabrics.

3. Use the leaf templates to cut four large leaves and four small leaves from each of the three green fabrics for a total of 12 large leaves and 12 small leaves.

Making the Flower Blocks

1. Iron the flower shapes, leaves, and background squares, applying spray starch for stability while sewing. Fold each background square in half vertically and then horizontally, right sides together, and lightly press the folds to mark the centers. Repeat with the flower shapes, referring to the cutting lines on the pattern as a guide.

2. For each of the eight flower units, select one large, one medium, and one small flower shape from the same color family that work well together. Center a large flower on each background square, using the fold lines as a guide, and pin in place. Stitch around each flower, ¼" from the raw edge. Cut away the background fabric behind the large flower on each appliqué, leaving a ¼" seam allowance. Place the medium flower for each unit over the large flower as desired. Stitch ¼" from the raw edge and then cut away the large flower fabric behind the medium flower appliqué as before. Position and stitch the small flower for each unit over the medium flower as desired. Cut away the medium flower fabric behind the

small flower appliqué. Press the units from the wrong side.

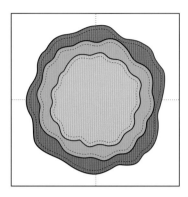

3. Use a rotary cutter and ruler to cut each appliquéd square into quarters, following the fold lines.

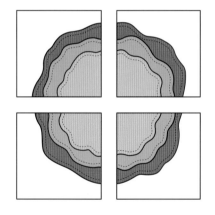

4. Select one quarter square from each of the four color families for each block. When you are satisfied with all of the arrangements, stitch the quarters together to form a new square. Press the seams open.

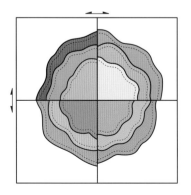

5. Press each block. Square up each block to 11".

Assembling the Quilt Top

1. Refer to the quilt assembly diagram to arrange the blocks into four horizontal rows of two blocks each. Stitch the blocks in each row together. Stitch the rows together.

2. Measure the quilt top through the vertical and horizontal centers. Record the measurements. Refer to "Step 8: Add the Borders" on page 13 for information on piecing and cutting the border strips to the *recorded* lengths. Stitch the side borders to the quilt sides. Sew a corner square to the ends of each top and bottom border strip. Stitch the strips to the top and bottom edges of the quilt top.

3. Press the quilt top.

Finishing

Refer to "Finishing Your Quilt" on pages 15–17.

1. Layer the quilt top with backing and batting; baste.

2. Quilt just outside the raw edge of each flower piece in each block. Begin with the small flower in each block and end with the large flower. Quilt the blocks in the center of the quilt first and work toward the outer edges. When all of the flowers are quilted, meander quilt or stipple quilt the background.

3. Arrange the leaves around the flowers as desired. Refer to the photo on page 18 if necessary.

4. Stitch around each leaf ¼" from the raw edge, stopping with the needle down when you are two-thirds of the way around the leaf. Lift the presser foot and gently insert a small amount of fiberfill into the leaf. Lower the presser foot and finish stitching around the leaf. If desired,

straight stitch from the base of the leaf halfway to the tip to create a vein.

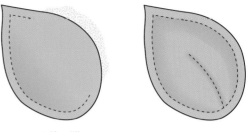

Insert fiberfill.

5. Glue or hand stitch the petals to the centers of each flower, or sew buttons to the flower centers.

6. Bind the quilt edges.

7. Add a hanging sleeve and label.

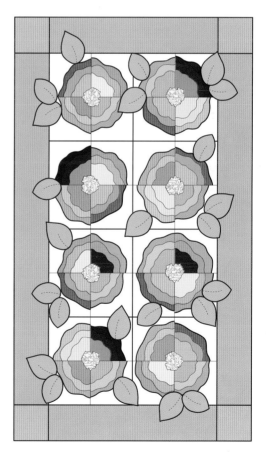

Quilt Assembly Diagram

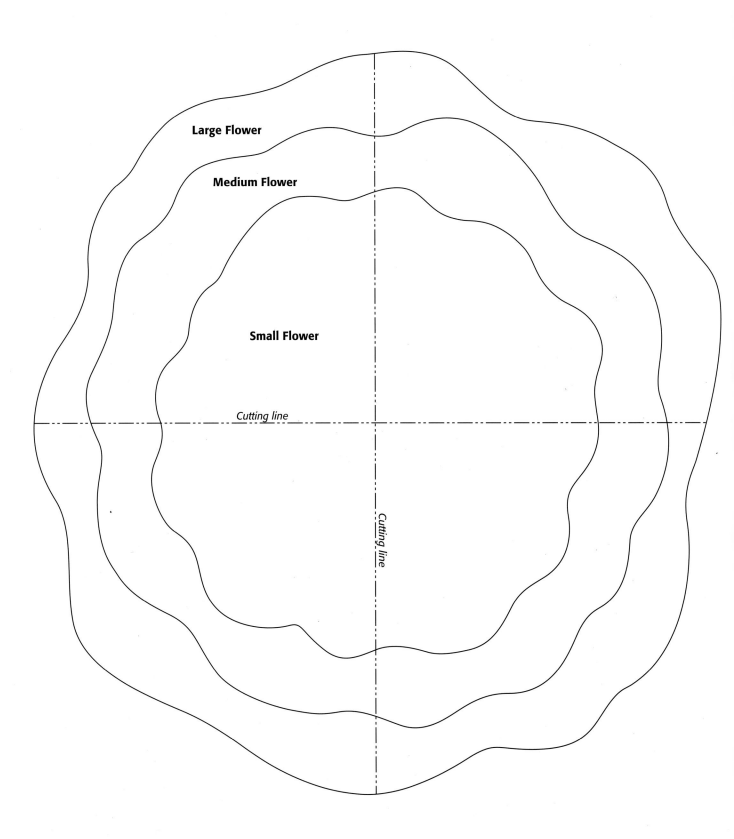

Large Flower

Medium Flower

Small Flower

Cutting line

Cutting line

Enlarge patterns 133%.

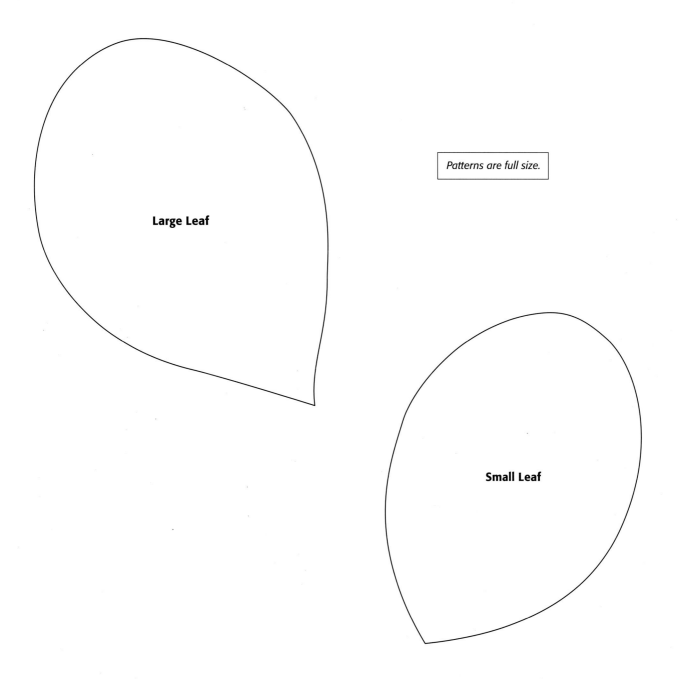

Large Leaf

Patterns are full size.

Small Leaf

HEARTBREAKER

Finished Quilt Size: 55" x 69"
Finished Block Size: 12" x 12½"

Pieced by Joan Segna and Jayme Crow. Machine quilted by Sandy Sims, Heirloom Originals.

What little girl doesn't grow up drawing hearts as the dot of an *i*, using a heart shape as a symbol for love, and of course, drawing a heart around her and her first heartthrob's initials. Hearts are the stuff dreams are made of!

Materials

Yardage is based on 42"-wide fabric.

- 1⅛ yards of red for outer border
- ⅞ yard of light pink for block backgrounds
- ⅞ yard of light lavender for block backgrounds
- ⅞ yard of purple for inner border
- 10" x 11½" rectangle *each* of 6 different fabrics from the red family for large swirl hearts
- 10" x 11½" rectangle *each* of 6 different fabrics from the purple family for large swirl hearts
- 8" x 8" square *each* of 16 different fabrics from the red and purple families for medium hearts
- 5½" x 6" rectangle *each* of 16 different fabrics from the red and purple families for small hearts
- 3½" x 4" rectangle *each* of 16 different fabrics from the red and purple families for center hearts
- 3½ yards of fabric for backing
- ⅝ yard of fabric for binding
- 63" x 77" piece of batting
- 4 yards of 12"-wide paper-backed fusible web
- Freezer paper
- Spray starch

Cutting

All measurements include ¼"-wide seam allowances.

From the fusible web, cut:
12 rectangles, 10" x 11½"

From the light pink, cut:
4 strips, 6½" x 42"; crosscut the strips into
    12 rectangles, 6½" x 13"

From the light lavender, cut:
4 strips, 6½" x 42"; crosscut the strips into
    12 rectangles, 6½" x 13"

From the purple for the inner border, cut:
5 strips, 4½" x 42"

From the red for the outer border, cut:
6 strips, 6" x 42"

From the backing fabric, cut:
2 pieces, 42" x 63"

From the binding fabric, cut:
7 strips, 2¼" x 42"

Cutting the Hearts

1. Enlarge the large swirl heart pattern on page 29 by the percentage indicated. Using the enlarged pattern, center and trace one heart onto the paper side of each fusible-web rectangle. Follow the manufacturer's instructions to fuse each fusible-web square to the wrong side of the assorted purple and assorted red 10" x 11½" rectangles. Cut out the swirl hearts on the traced lines, cutting along the outside edges of each heart first. Then cut along the inner edges as indicated on the pattern. Set the swirls aside.

2. Trace the medium, small, and center heart patterns on page 28 onto freezer paper and cut them out.

3. Use the medium heart template to cut one shape from each of the 16 medium heart fabrics. Repeat with the small and center heart templates and the appropriate fabrics. Separate the medium, small, and center heart shapes by size and set them aside.

Making the Heart Blocks

1. Sew each light pink 6½" x 13" rectangle to a light lavender 6½" x 13" rectangle along the long edges to make the block backgrounds. Press the seams open.

2. Arrange the block backgrounds into four horizontal rows of three blocks each so that the pink and lavender halves of the blocks alternate from row to row as shown in the quilt assembly diagram on page 27. Do not sew the blocks together at this time.

3. Temporarily position a swirl heart on the center of each block, alternating the red and purple hearts in each row. When you are satisfied with the arrangement, pin the hearts to the blocks and label each block with its position in the quilt (such as "row 1, block 1").

4. For each block, carefully remove the paper backing from the swirl heart. Be careful not to stretch the fabric as you remove the paper. Center the swirl heart, fusible side down, on the right side of the block. Position the heart so that the inverted point at the center top is about 2" from the top edge of the block. Follow the manufacturer's instructions to fuse the heart in place. If desired, edge stitch around each heart swirl.

TIP

Place the swirl heart pattern on a light box. Then position the background block on top of the pattern. Use the pattern as a guide to help arrange the heart on the block.

---

5. Iron the medium, small, and center hearts, applying spray starch for stability while sewing. Fold the medium and small hearts in half vertically, right sides together, and press the folds to mark the centers.

6. For each of the 16 heart units, select one medium and one small heart shape that work well together. Center the small heart on the medium heart, using the folds as a guide; pin in place. Stitch around the small heart, ⅛" from the edge. Cut away the medium heart fabric behind the small heart, leaving a ¼" seam allowance.

7. Use a rotary cutter and ruler to cut the units in half through the vertical center, following the fold lines. Mark the left halves "side A" and the right halves "side B." Set the half-units aside.

Assembling the Quilt Top

1. Arrange the blocks into rows as previously determined.

2. Position a side-A heart half-unit upside down on the left side of each block. Align the cut edges with the block raw edges and position the top of each heart 1½" from the block bottom edge as shown; pin in place. Repeat with the right side of each block, placing the top of a side-B heart half-unit 2" from the block bottom edge.

3. Stitch along the previous stitching of each small heart half. Stitch ⅛" from the edge of each medium heart. Do not remove the fabric from behind the hearts. Set aside the remaining heart half-units to be used for the inner border.

4. Stitch the blocks in each row together. Press the seams open.

5. Position a center heart in the center of each of the eight completed split hearts. Stitch ⅛" from the edges of each center heart.

6. Stitch the rows together. Press the seams in one direction.

7. Measure the quilt top for borders as instructed in "Step 8: Add the Borders" on page 13. Piece and cut the inner side border strips to the required length. Referring to the quilt assembly diagram, lay one border strip flush with the right edge of the quilt top, matching the top and bottom edges. Position four of the remaining heart half-units flush with the border strip inner edges so they complete the remaining block half-units; pin in place. Repeat with the left border strip. Stitch along the previous stitching of each small and medium heart half-unit. Stitch the borders to the sides of the quilt top, matching the heart half-units. Press the seams open. Position a center heart in the center of each of the completed border hearts. Stitch ⅛" from the edges of each center heart.

8. Cut the top and bottom inner border strips to the required length and stitch them to the top and bottom edges of the quilt top.

9. Measure the quilt top for outer borders. Piece and cut the outer side border strips to the required length and stitch them to the quilt sides. Cut the top and bottom outer border strips to the required length and stitch them to the top and bottom edges of the quilt top.

10. Press the quilt top.

Finishing

Refer to "Finishing Your Quilt" on pages 15–17.

1. Layer the quilt top with backing and batting; baste.

2. Quilt around each of the small split hearts to stabilize the quilt. Use a meandering stitch to quilt the block backgrounds and borders. Vary the size of the stitch to suit the area and to add interest to the quilt.

3. Bind the quilt edges.

4. Add a hanging sleeve and label.

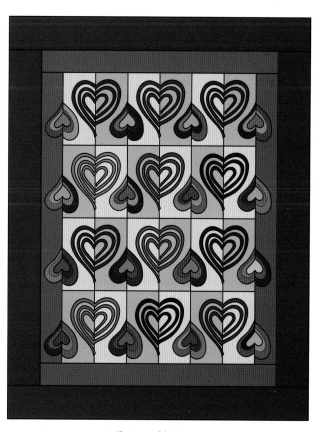

Quilt Assembly Diagram

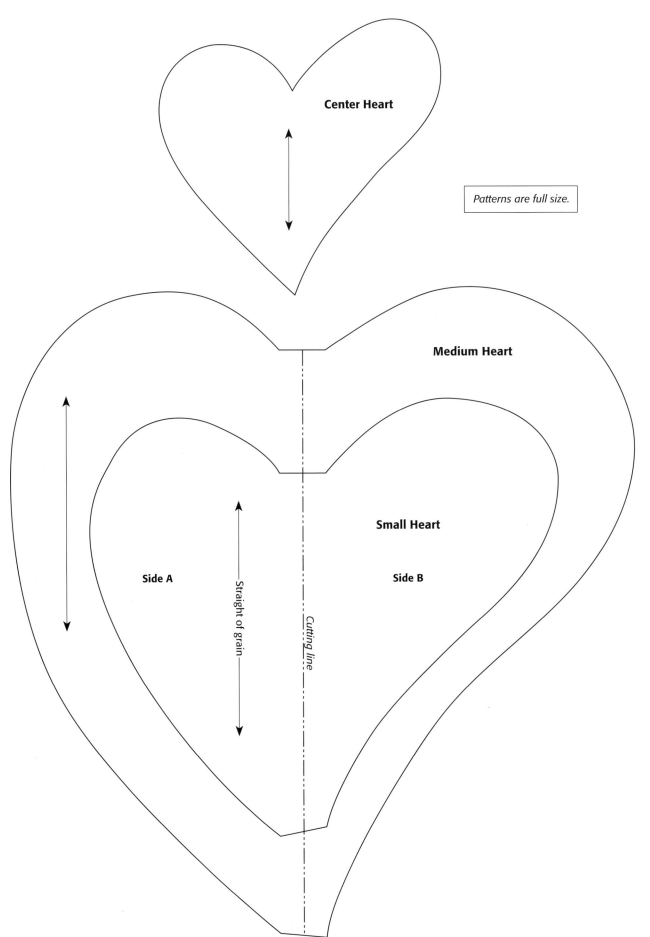

Center Heart

Patterns are full size.

Medium Heart

Small Heart

Side A

Straight of grain

Cutting line

Side B

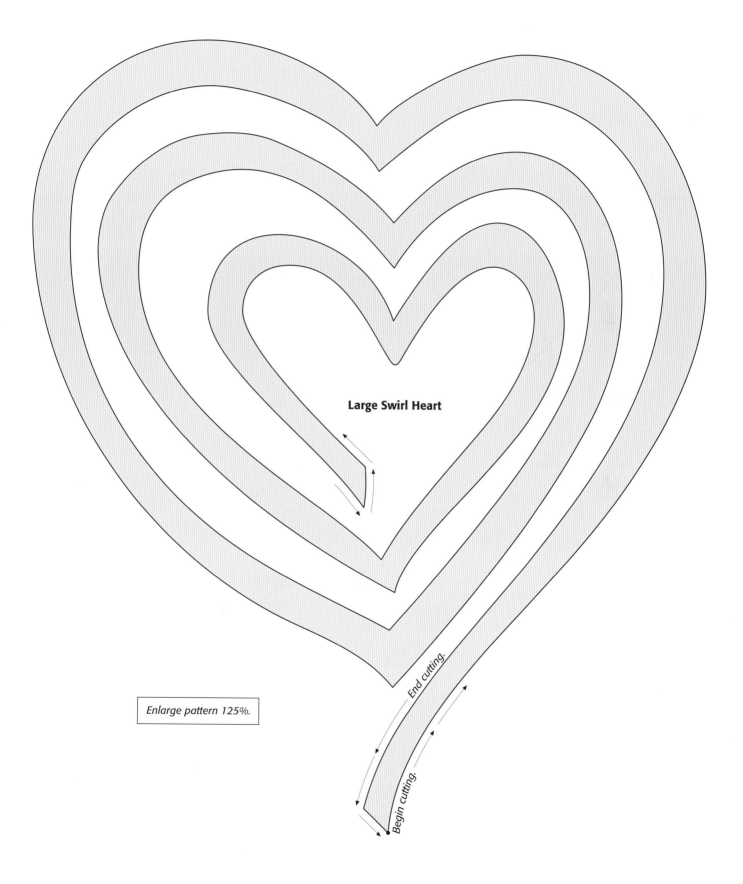

Large Swirl Heart

Enlarge pattern 125%.

End cutting.

Begin cutting.

FIELD OF SUNFLOWERS

Finished Quilt Size: 37½" x 48½"

Pieced by Joan Segna and Jayme Crow. Machine quilted by Sandy Sims, Heirloom Originals.

While I was in the hospital recuperating from the birth of my third child, a friend of mine came to visit. I knew that her budget was tight, so imagine my surprise when she handed me a big bouquet of sunflowers! A smile creased her warm, sunny face as I read the tag on the flowers: Donated by the Texas Department of Highways. It made my day!

—Joan

Materials

Yardage is based on 42"-wide fabric.

- ❖ ¾ yard of blue for sky
- ❖ ½ yard of green #1 for field
- ❖ ½ yard of green #2 for stems
- ❖ ⅝ yard of brown for outer border
- ❖ ¼ yard of tan check for inner border
- ❖ 1 fat quarter *each* of 3 different fabrics from the green family for leaves
- ❖ 11" x 12" rectangle *each* of 7 different fabrics from the yellow family for large flowers
- ❖ 10" x 11" rectangle *each* of 7 different fabrics from the yellow family for medium flowers
- ❖ 8" x 9" rectangle *each* of 7 different fabrics from the yellow family for small flowers
- ❖ 5" x 5½" rectangle *each* of 7 different fabrics from the brown family for flower centers
- ❖ 1¾ yards of fabric for backing
- ❖ ½ yard of fabric for binding
- ❖ 42" x 54" piece of batting
- ❖ 1½ yards of 18"-wide paper-backed fusible web
- ❖ Rayon threads: yellow, brown, blue, light green
- ❖ Monofilament thread
- ❖ 7 yards of ½"-wide paper-backed fusible-web tape or basting glue (optional)
- ❖ 7 black 1¾"-diameter buttons for flower centers
- ❖ Green bugle beads and seed beads for flower stem and leaf vein accents
- ❖ Freezer paper
- ❖ Spray starch

Cutting

All measurements include ¼"-wide seam allowances.

From the green #1, cut:
1 rectangle, 14" x 42"

From the blue, cut:
1 rectangle, 22" x 42"

From the fusible web, cut:
3 squares, 18" x 18"

From the tan check, cut:
4 strips, 1½" x 42"

From the brown, cut:
5 strips, 3" x 42"

From the backing fabric, cut:
1 piece, 42" x 54"

From the binding fabric, cut:
5 strips, 2¼" x 42"

Assembling the Quilt Background

1. Refer to the photo on page 30 to cut gently rolling curves along one long edge of the green #1 rectangle.
2. Place the curved edge of the green rectangle over one long edge of the blue rectangle; pin in place. Set your machine for a feather stitch and thread the needle and bobbin with green rayon thread. Stitch ¼" from the curved raw edge of the green rectangle. Turn the pieced background to the wrong side and trim the blue fabric ¼" from the seam line; press.
3. Trim the background rectangle to 31" x 42", leaving a larger portion of sky than field.
4. Refer to "Layering and Basting" on page 15 to center the background on the backing and batting. Pin-baste the layers together. The borders will be added later, so do not trim away the excess batting and backing at this time.
5. With your machine still set for a feather stitch and threaded with green thread, stitch rows of curved lines across the field, following the curve at the upper edge and stitching through

all of the layers. Space the rows about 2" apart and occasionally exaggerate the curves for interest. Rethread your machine with blue thread and use a meandering stitch to quilt the sky portion of the background.

Cutting the Sunflower Pieces

1. Enlarge the sunflower patterns on page 34 and the leaf patterns on page 35 by the percentages indicated. Trace the sunflower patterns onto freezer paper and cut them out.

2. Use the large sunflower template to cut one shape from each of the seven large-sunflower fabrics. Repeat with the medium, small, and center sunflower templates and the appropriate fabrics.

3. Using the enlarged leaf patterns, trace leaf A onto the paper side of a fusible web square six times. Repeat to trace leaves B and C onto the remaining two squares of fusible web, tracing a different leaf on each square six times. Refer to the manufacturer's instructions to fuse one square to the wrong side of each of the three green fat quarters. Cut out the leaves on the marked lines and set them aside.

4. From the stem fabric, use your scissors to freehand cut five stems, approximately ¾" x 42". Cut two additional stems, but curve the end of one to the left and the other to the right, referring to the photo if necessary. The stems will look more natural if you cut them by hand rather than with a rotary cutter. Some unevenness in width is fine. If they're not perfectly straight, that's OK too. You can position the leaves to cover any irregularities you don't want visible.

Assembling the Flowers

1. Iron the large, medium, small, and center sunflower shapes, applying spray starch for stability while sewing. Fold the pieces in half vertically and horizontally, right sides together, and press the folds to mark the centers.

2. For each of the seven sunflower units, select one large, one medium, and one small sunflower shape and one flower center that work well together. Center the medium sunflower shape from each unit on the large sunflower shape from the same unit, using the folds as a guide; pin in place. Thread your machine with yellow rayon thread and stitch around each medium sunflower, ¼" from the edge. Cut out the large sunflower fabric behind the medium sunflower appliqués, leaving a ¼" seam allowance. Center and stitch the small flower from each unit on the medium sunflower; cut away the medium sunflower fabric behind the small sunflower appliqués. Center and stitch the sunflower center from each unit on the small sunflower; cut away the small sunflower fabric behind each center appliqué. Press the appliqué units from the wrong side.

3. Using a rotary cutter and ruler, cut each appliqué unit into quarters, following the fold lines.

4. Select four different sunflower quarters for the new units. When you are satisfied with all of the arrangements, stitch the quarters together. Press the seams open.

Adding the Sunflowers and Borders

1. Referring to the quilt assembly diagram, temporarily pin the sunflower units to the background, extending some beyond the background so they will overlap onto the borders.

2. Place a stem under each sunflower head and extend it to the bottom edge. Make any necessary adjustments to the flowers and stems and then pin the stems in place. Cut off any excess stem so that the stem end is flush with the bottom edge of the quilt background. Remove the sunflower heads. Pin any stems that extend past the background top and side edges out of the way so they will not be caught in the border seams; the bottoms of the stems will be caught in the bottom inner border seam.

3. Measure the quilt top for the inner side borders as instructed in "Step 8: Add the Borders" on page 13. Cut two of the inner border strips to the required length and stitch them to the quilt sides through all of the layers. Press the seams toward the borders. Measure the quilt top for the inner top and bottom borders. Using the remainder of the strips from the side borders and the remaining two inner border strips, piece and cut two strips to the required length and stitch them to the top and bottom edges of the quilt top, securing the stem ends at the bottom edge. Press the seams toward the borders. Repeat with the outer border strips, piecing and cutting as necessary to achieve the required length.

4. Press the quilt top.

Finishing

1. Secure the stems to the quilt top for stitching by either hand basting them in place or using fusible-web tape or fabric glue. With matching thread, use the machine buttonhole setting to stitch along the stems' long raw edges through all of the quilt layers.

2. Pin the sunflower heads back in place. Remove the paper backing from the leaves. Arrange the leaves on the stems, overlapping some onto the borders and tucking some under the flower heads. You have a few more leaves than necessary so that you have placement options. Follow the manufacturer's instructions to fuse the leaves in place.

3. Using monofilament thread, stitch in the ditch of each sunflower head's seams to secure them to the background. Then, follow the previous stitching on each flower layer, beginning with the flower center and working out. If desired, stitch around each leaf.

4. Hand stitch a button to the center of each sunflower head.

5. Hand stitch beads to each stem and along each leaf's vein as desired, referring to the photo as needed.

6. Refer to "Finishing Your Quilt" on pages 15–17 to bind the quilt edges and add a hanging sleeve and label.

Quilt Assembly Diagram

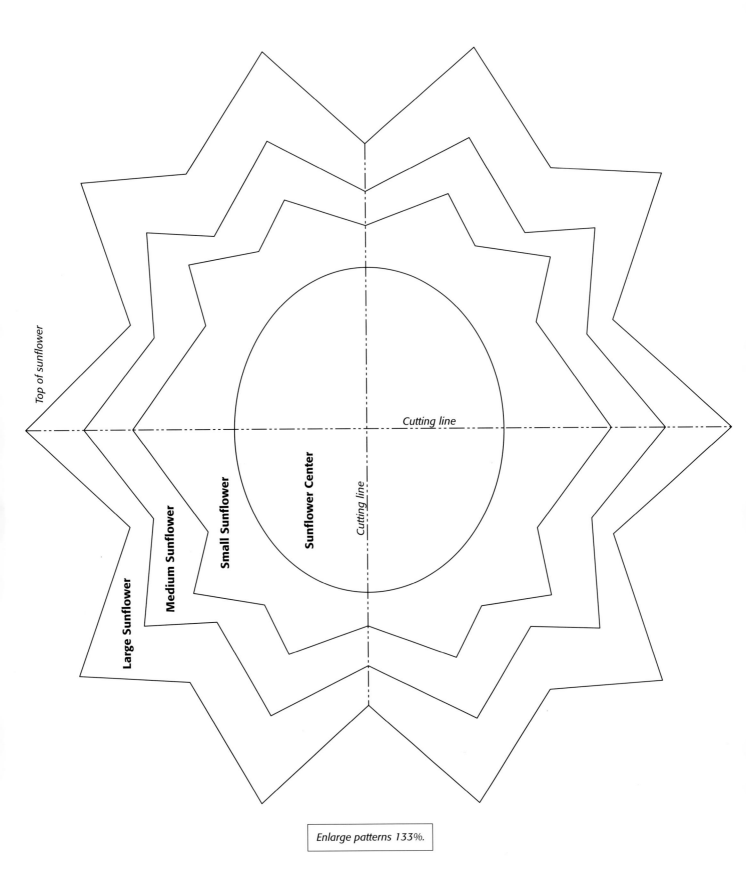

Top of sunflower

Cutting line

Cutting line

Sunflower Center

Small Sunflower

Medium Sunflower

Large Sunflower

Enlarge patterns 133%.

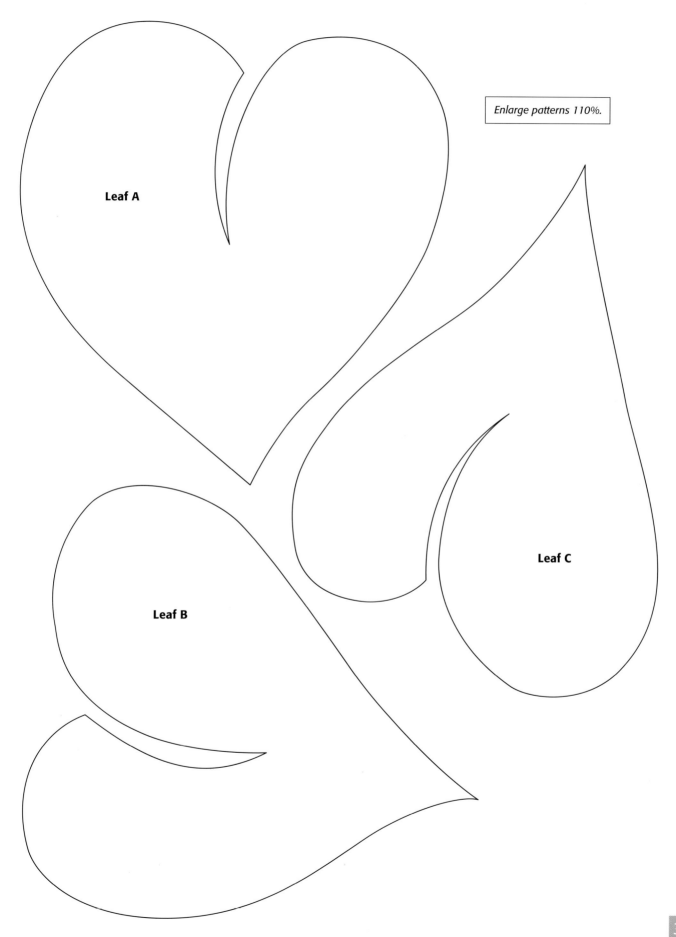

Enlarge patterns 110%.

Leaf A

Leaf B

Leaf C

PIECES OF AMERICANA

Finished Quilt Size: 35¾" x 47¾"
Finished Block Size: 10"

Pieced by Joan Segna. Machine quilted by Sandy Sims, Heirloom Originals.

Our little neighborhood of sixty homes always held a Fourth of July children's parade. Kids made floats from red wagons, decorated bicycles, and scavenged through past years' costumes for the chance to proudly march down the street. This patriotic wall hanging reminds me of the enthusiasm surrounding the day.

—Joan

Materials

Yardage is based on 42"-wide fabric.

❖ ¾ yard of red for inner border

❖ ⅝ yard of blue for block backgrounds and border hearts and star

❖ ⅝ yard of white for block backgrounds and border hearts

❖ ½ yard of blue-and-white stripe for outer border

❖ ¼ yard *each* of 2 different fabrics from the yellow family for sashing

❖ 10" x 11" rectangle *each* of 6 different fabrics from the red family for block large hearts

❖ 7½" x 8½" rectangle *each* of 6 different fabrics from the red family for block medium hearts

❖ 6" x 6½" rectangle *each* of 6 different fabrics from the yellow family for block stars

❖ 5" x 6" rectangle *each* of 2 different fabrics from the yellow family for border stars

❖ 5" x 6" rectangle of blue for border star

❖ 1¾ yards of fabric for backing

❖ ½ yard of fabric for binding

❖ 42" x 54" piece of batting

❖ 9" x 12" rectangle of paper-backed fusible web

Cutting

All measurements include ¼"-wide seam allowances.

From the blue for block backgrounds, cut:
10 strips, 1½" x 42"

From the white for block backgrounds, cut:
10 strips, 1½" x 42"

From *each* of the yellows for sashing, cut:
4 strips, 1½" x 42"; crosscut the strips into:
    6 strips, 1½" x 10½"
    6 strips, 1½" x 12½"

From the red for the inner border, cut:
2 strips, 6½" x 42"
2 strips, 2¼" x 42"

From the blue-and-white stripe, cut:
5 strips, 2½" x 42"

From the backing fabric, cut:
1 piece, 42" x 54"

From the binding fabric, cut:
5 strips, 2¼" x 42"

Assembling the Block Backgrounds

1. Alternately sew five blue strips and five white strips together along the long edges as shown to make a strip set. Press the seams in one direction. Make two. From the strip sets, crosscut 30 segments 1½" wide and 3 segments 11" wide. Set the 11"-wide segments aside for the stripe block backgrounds.

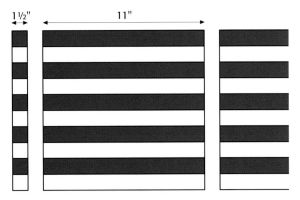

1½"   11"

Make 2 strip sets.
Cut 30 segments 1½" wide
and 3 segments 11" wide.

2. For the checkerboard block backgrounds, stitch five 1½"-wide segments together, reversing every other segment as shown. Make six.

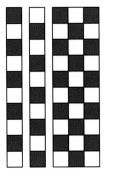

Make 6.

Cutting the Block Hearts and Stars

1. Referring to "Step 1: Make the Templates" on page 11, make full-size large and medium heart patterns, using the half-patterns on page 41. Trace the full-size large and medium heart patterns and the block-star pattern on page 41 onto freezer paper and cut them out.

2. Use the large heart template to cut one shape from each of the six large-heart fabrics. Repeat with the medium heart and block-star templates and the appropriate fabrics.

Making the Blocks

1. Iron the heart and star shapes, applying spray starch for stability while sewing. Fold each striped background rectangle, each large and medium heart, and each block star in half vertically, right sides together, and lightly press the folds to mark the centers.

2. Match the long edges of two checkerboard units, reversing one so that the pattern continues. From the wrong side, use transparent tape to join the units, making sure the edges are butted against each other, not overlapped.

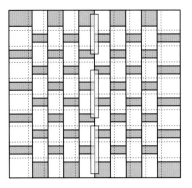

3. Center a large heart on each stripe and checkerboard background, using the center folds and the taped edges as a guide; pin in place. Stitch around each heart, ¼" from the raw edges. Cut away the background fabric behind each large heart appliqué, leaving approximately a ¼" seam allowance. Set aside the cut-away portions for the border hearts.

Center a medium heart on each large heart; pin in place. Stitch ¼" from the raw edges, and then cut away the large heart fabric behind each medium heart appliqué as before. Save the hearts for use in "Tug at Your Heart" on page 43, if desired. Center and stitch a star over each medium heart. *Do not cut away the fabric behind the star.*

4. Using your rotary cutter and ruler, cut the striped background blocks in half, following the fold lines as a guide. Cut the checkerboard background blocks in half, following the taped "seam." Remove the tape.

5. Select one striped block half and one checkerboard block half to make one block. When satisfied with all of the block arrangements, stitch the halves together. Press the seams open.

Assembling the Quilt Top

1. Arrange the blocks into three horizontal rows of two blocks each. Label the blocks 1–6 as shown. Using yellow sashing strips cut from the same fabric, stitch the 1½" x 10½" strips to the top and bottom edges of blocks 1, 4, and 5. Stitch the 1½" x 12½" strips to the sides of the blocks. Stitch the remaining sashing strips to blocks 2, 3, and 6 in the same manner.

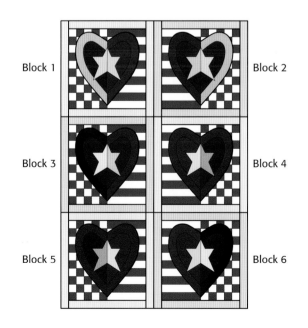

2. Stitch the blocks in each row together. Sew the rows together.

3. Measure the quilt top for the inner right border as instructed in "Step 8: Add the Borders" on page 13. Cut a red 6½"-wide strip to the required length and stitch it to the right edge of the quilt top. Measure the quilt top for the inner bottom border, cut the remaining 6½"-wide strip to the required length, and stitch it to the bottom of the quilt top. Repeat this process for the left border and then the top border, using the 2¼"-wide strips, piecing and cutting as necessary to achieve the required length.

4. Measure the quilt top for the outer borders. Piece and cut the side outer border strips to the required length and stitch them to the quilt sides. Piece and cut the top and bottom outer border strips to the required length and stitch them to the top and bottom edges of the quilt top.

5. Trace the border heart pattern on page 42 onto freezer paper and cut it out.

6. Using the striped and checkerboard hearts that were cut away from the block backgrounds, sew two checkerboard heart halves together to make one heart. Repeat to make one more heart. Cut one striped heart in half vertically; sew each half to a checkerboard half. Use the freezer-paper template to trim the joined hearts and the two striped hearts to size.

7. Follow the manufacturer's instructions to trace the border star pattern on page 42 onto the paper side of the fusible web three times. Cut out the traced stars approximately ⅛" from the lines. Fuse one star to each of the yellow and the blue 5" x 6" rectangles. Cut out the stars on the traced lines and remove the paper backing.

8. Referring to the photo on page 36 or the quilt assembly diagram, arrange the hearts and stars on the borders. Fuse the stars in place, following the manufacturer's instructions. Hand or machine appliqué the hearts in place using a decorative stitch.

9. Press the quilt top.

Finishing

Refer to "Finishing Your Quilt" on pages 15–17.

1. Layer the quilt top with backing and batting.

2. Quilt around the outside raw edge of each small heart. Begin with the blocks in the center row of the quilt and work toward the outer edges. Quilt in the ditch of the block-background seams and along the sashing seams. Quilt around the stars in the border. Quilt in the ditch of the border hearts, and then use a meandering star motif to stitch in the open spaces of the inner borders. Stitch along the stripes of the outer border.

3. Bind the quilt edges.

4. Add a hanging sleeve and label.

Quilt Assembly Diagram

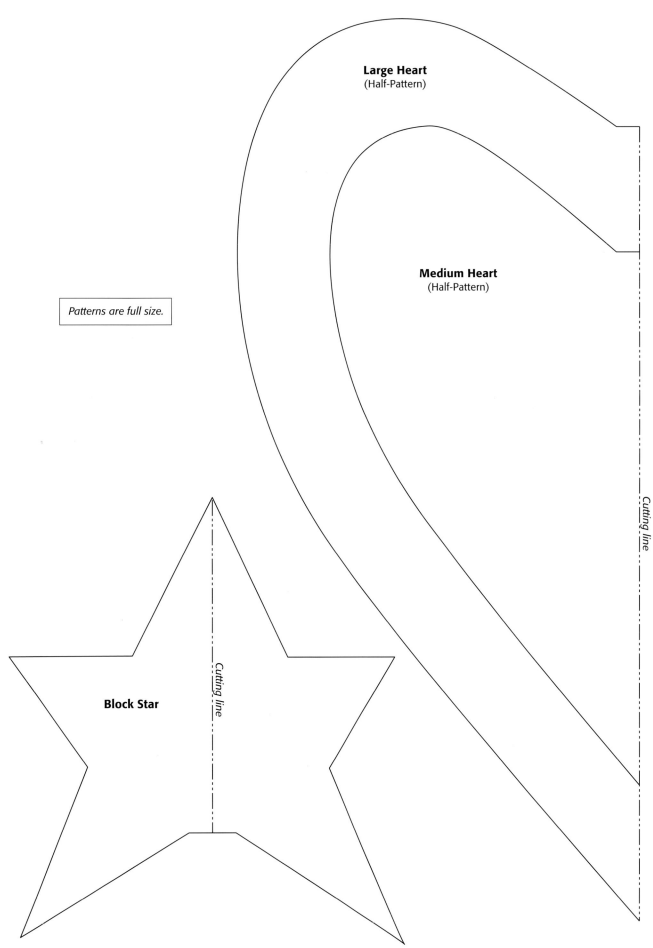

Large Heart
(Half-Pattern)

Medium Heart
(Half-Pattern)

Patterns are full size.

Cutting line

Block Star

Cutting line

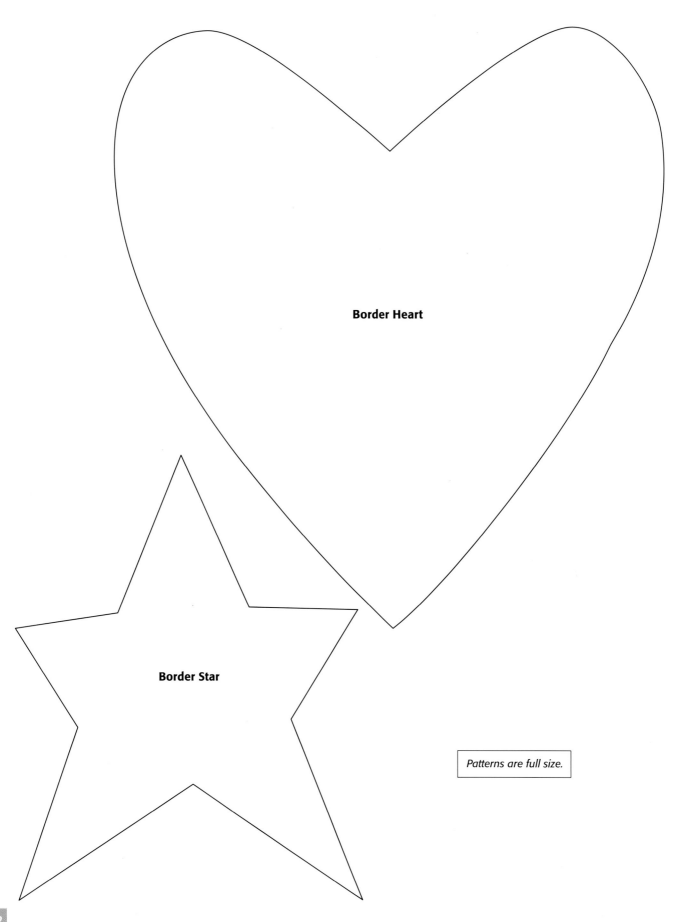

Border Heart

Border Star

Patterns are full size.

TUG AT YOUR HEART

Finished Quilt Size: 8" x 23½"

By Joan Segna.

Greet summer with this welcoming red-white-and-blue bell pull. It's sure to bring back memories of lemonade stands, lightning bugs, camping, and lots of family fun.

Materials

Yardage is based on 42"-wide fabric.

- ❖ ¼ yard of yellow for flanged inner border

- ❖ ¼ yard of blue-and-white stripe for outer border

- ❖ 1 fat quarter of navy blue for center background stripes, hanging loop, and bottom border

- ❖ 1 fat eighth of white for center background stripes

- ❖ 6" x 6" square *each* of 3 different fabrics from the red family for hearts *or* three cut-away hearts left over from "Pieces of Americana" (page 36)

- ❖ 8" x 21" piece of fabric for backing

- ❖ 8" x 21" piece of batting

- ❖ 4" x 8" piece of fusible medium-weight interfacing

- ❖ ¾ yard of narrow red rickrack

- ❖ Assorted buttons for embellishing hearts

- ❖ Yellow, textured 2-ply yarn for tassel or 3"-long purchased tassel

- ❖ 1"- to 1½"-long bell

- ❖ 12"-wide bell-pull hanger

- ❖ Freezer paper

- ❖ Spray starch

Cutting

All measurements include ¼"-wide seam allowances.

From the navy blue, cut:
3 strips, 1½" x 22"
1 rectangle, 2½" x 8½"

From the white, cut:
3 strips, 1½" x 22"

From the yellow, cut:
2 strips, 1½" x 42"

From the blue-and-white stripe, cut:
2 strips, 2" x 42"

From the fusible interfacing, cut:
1 rectangle, 1" x 8"

Assembling the Bell Pull

1. Alternately stitch the navy and white strips together along the long edges as shown to make a strip set. Press the seams in one direction. Crosscut the strip set into three segments, 6½" wide.

Make 1 strip set.
Cut 3 segments.

2. Stitch the segments together along the short edges as shown to continue the stripe pattern. Set the background piece aside.

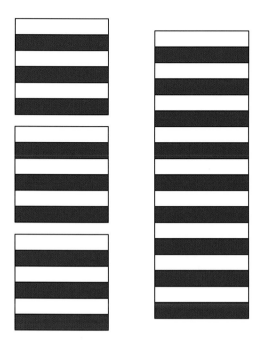

3. Trace the heart pattern on page 47 onto freezer paper and cut it out.

4. Use the template to cut one shape from each of the three red squares, or, if you made the "Pieces of Americana" project, cut from the leftover hearts. Fold each heart in half vertically, and lightly press the fold to mark the center. Using your rotary cutter and ruler, cut each heart in half on the center line. Stitch each heart half together with a different heart half. Press the seams open.

5. Iron the hearts, applying spray starch for stability while stitching.

6. Place the hearts in a vertical row through the center of the background piece. Leave an equal amount of space at the top and bottom of the background and an equal amount of space between each heart. Pin the hearts in place. Stitch around each heart, ¼" from the raw edges. Cut away the background fabric behind each heart, leaving a ¼" seam allowance. Press the piece from the wrong side.

7. Sew the ends of the yellow strips together with a bias seam to make one long strip. Trim the seam to ¼" and press it open. Press the strip in half lengthwise, wrong sides together. Cut off the selvage ends.

8. Refer to "Binding" on page 15 to stitch the strip to the edges of the background piece, mitering the corners. Do not fold the strip to the back and stitch it in place.

9. Measure the quilt top for borders as instructed in "Step 8: Add the Borders" on page 13. Cut the striped strips to the required length for the side borders and stitch them to the sides of the quilt top. Cut the top and bottom borders to the required length and stitch them to the top and bottom edges of the quilt top. Press the yellow strips toward the outer border. If desired, tack the corners of the yellow strips to keep them in place.

Finishing
Refer to "Finishing Your Quilt" on pages 15–17.

1. Center the quilt top on the batting and backing; baste. The side borders will extend beyond the batting at this time but will be turned under and stitched to the backing later.

2. Stitch in the ditch of the background seams. Quilt around each heart, following the previous stitching line.

3. Turn under ½" of the side borders to the quilt backing. Turn under the raw edge of each side border ¼" and hand stitch it in place.

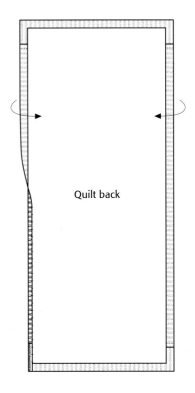

Quilt back

4. Trace the bottom border template on page 47 onto freezer paper and cut it out. Using the template, cut two shapes from the remaining navy blue fabric and one from the remaining interfacing. Trim the interfacing shape ¼" narrower than the template on each side.

5. Center the bottom border interfacing on the wrong side of one bottom border fabric. Follow the manufacturer's instructions to fuse it in place. Place the bottom border pieces right sides together; stitch ¼" from the ends and along the curved edge, leaving the straight edge open. Clip the curved edge; turn the piece to the right sides, and press.

6. Align the bottom border straight edge with the outer border raw edge as shown. Stitch

through the bottom two layers only, leaving the top layer of the bottom border free.

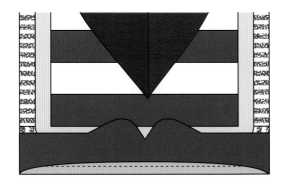

7. Fold down the bottom border piece. Turn under the seam allowance on the unstitched edge and hand stitch it to the backing, enclosing the seam allowance.

8. Center the 1" x 8" interfacing piece on one-half of the blue 2½" x 8½" rectangle. Follow the manufacturer's instructions to fuse it in place. Turn the blue rectangle sides under ¼" and stitch them in place.

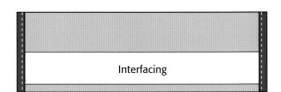

Interfacing

9. With right sides together, align the long edge of the rectangle without the interfacing with the top outer border; stitch. Press the remaining long raw edge under ¼". Fold it to the backing and hand stitch it to the quilt backing so it just covers the previous stitching and makes a pocket for inserting the hanger.

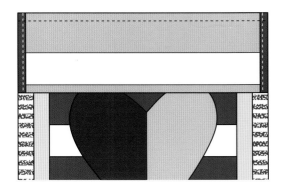

10. Cut two pieces of rickrack 1" longer than the width of the bell pull. Position each piece in place over the seam line between the top and bottom borders and the outer borders, wrapping ½" to the back on each side. Topstitch the rickrack in place.

11. Stitch the buttons to the hearts as desired.

12. Make a 3"-long tassel from the yellow yarn. Cut a 7"-long piece of yarn and insert it through the opening at the top of the bell. Secure the ends of the yarn inside the tassel. Tack the tassel in place at the center of the bottom border. Insert the bell-pull hanger through the top border opening.

13. Add a label.

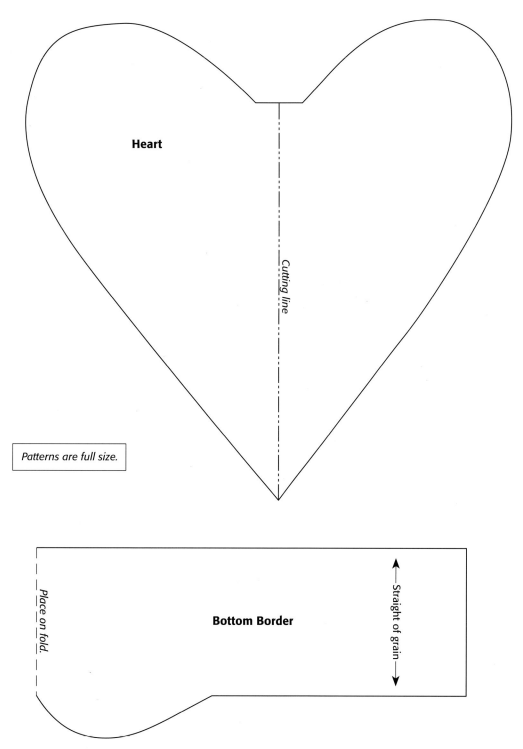

Heart

Cutting line

Patterns are full size.

Place on fold.

Bottom Border

Straight of grain

CRÈME BARTLETT

Finished Quilt Size: 35" x 56½"
Finished Block Size: 12½" x 15½"

Pieced by Joan Segna and Jayme Crow. Machine quilted by Sandy Sims, Heirloom Originals.

I grew up in Washington's Walla Walla Valley in the 1960s, and Mom canned quarts and quarts of fruit, one of which was the dreaded pear. Each pear had to be hand peeled, and I can still hear my mother saying "be careful not to bruise them." The center stringy piece had to be cut out with a knife in a "V"-cut and then the seeds scooped out with a melon-ball tool. But when winter came, I was always glad we had canned pears to put in green Jell-O or heap with a spoonful of cottage cheese.

— Jayme

Materials

Yardage is based on 42"-wide fabric.

- ✦ 1 yard of dark brown for border

- ✦ ⅝ yard of off-white for appliqué backgrounds

- ✦ 1 fat quarter *each* of 2 different golds, 2 different yellow-greens, and 2 different rusts for block backgrounds

- ✦ 7½" x 10" rectangle *each* of 2 different dark golds, 2 different dark yellow-greens, and 2 different dark rusts for large pears

- ✦ 6" x 9" rectangle *each* of 2 different medium golds, 2 different medium yellow-greens, and 2 different medium rusts for medium pears

- ✦ 4" x 6" rectangle *each* of 2 different light golds, 2 different light yellow-greens, and 2 different light rusts for small pears

- ✦ 5" x 5" square of medium brown for pear stems

- ✦ 2 yards of fabric for backing

- ✦ ½ yard of fabric for binding

- ✦ 42" x 64" piece of batting

- ✦ 5" x 5" square of paper-backed fusible web

- ✦ 1⅛ yards of 2"-wide variegated green silk ribbon for leaves

- ✦ Matching metallic and rayon threads for stitching and quilting

- ✦ Freezer paper

- ✦ Spray starch

- ✦ Seam sealant (optional)

- ✦ Fabric glue (optional)

Cutting

All measurements include ¼"-wide seam allowances.

From the off-white, cut:
6 rectangles, 9" x 12"

From *each* of the six fat quarters, cut:
1 rectangle, 13" x 16"

From the dark brown, cut:
5 strips, 5½" x 42"

From the backing fabric, cut:
1 piece, 42" x 64"

From the binding fabric, cut:
5 strips, 2¼" x 42"

Cutting the Pear Shapes

1. Trace the large, medium, and small pear patterns on page 52 onto freezer paper and cut them out.

2. Use the large pear template to cut one shape from each of the six large-pear fabrics. Repeat with the medium and small pear templates and the appropriate fabrics.

Making the Blocks

1. On each off-white rectangle, mark a dot on the rectangle top edge 6" from the top left corner; mark another dot on the rectangle bottom edge 3½" from the bottom left corner. Using a sharp pencil and ruler, draw a line to connect the two dots. This will be your cutting line. Mark 1½" up from the bottom edge of the line as a placement guide for the large pear.

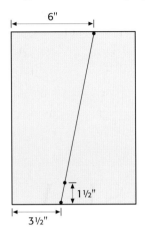

2. Iron the pear shapes, applying spray starch for stability while sewing. Fold the shapes in half vertically, right sides together, and lightly press the folds to mark the centers.

3. For each of the six pear units, select one small, medium, and large pear from the same color family. Align the fold line of each large pear on the marked line of a white rectangle and place the bottom of the pear at the 1½" mark. Pin in place. With your machine set for the decorative stitch of your choice and threaded with a matching rayon thread, stitch around each pear, ⅛" from the raw edge. Cut away the background fabric behind each pear, leaving a ¼" seam allowance. Center the medium pear shape from each unit on the large pear; pin in place. Stitch ⅛" from the raw edge and then cut away the large pear fabric behind the medium pear appliqués as before. Referring to the photo on page 48, position the small pear from each unit toward the bottom of the medium pear; pin in place. Cut away the medium pear behind the small pear appliqués. Press the units from the wrong side.

4. Using a rotary cutter and ruler, cut apart each pear unit on the marked line.

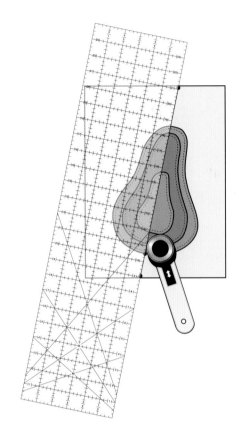

5. Stitch the left half of one gold pear to the right half of the other gold pear and vise versa. Repeat with the yellow-green pear halves and the rust pear halves. Press the seams open.

6. Trim each unit to 8½" x 11". To round the corners of each unit, trace the corner pattern on page 52 onto freezer paper and cut it out. Iron the template to each corner of each unit; cut away the excess beyond the curved edge of the template.

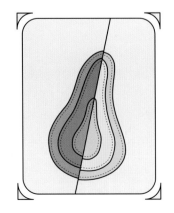

7. Select a 13" x 16" block background rectangle that works well with each pear unit. Center each pear unit on the right side of the selected rectangle; pin in place. With your machine set for a straight stitch, stitch ⅛" from the edges of each pear unit. Turn the rectangle to the wrong side and cut away the block background rectangle behind the pear unit background, leaving a ¼" seam allowance.

Assembling the Quilt Top

1. Refer to the quilt assembly diagram to arrange the blocks into three horizontal rows of two blocks each as desired. Stitch the blocks in each row together. Sew the rows together.

2. Measure the quilt top for borders as instructed in "Step 8: Add the Borders" on page 13. Piece and cut the side border strips to the required length and stitch them to the quilt top. Cut the top and bottom borders to the required length and stitch them to the top and bottom edges of the quilt top.

3. Trace the stem pattern on page 52 onto the paper side of the fusible-web square six times. Follow the manufacturer's instructions to fuse the web square to the wrong side of the brown fabric square. Cut out the stems on the marked lines and remove the paper backing. Place a stem at the top of each pear and fuse it in place.

Finishing

Refer to "Finishing Your Quilt" on pages 15–17.

1. Layer the quilt top with backing and batting; baste.

2. Using rayon and metallic threads as desired, quilt ⅛" from the edges of each pear shape. Echo quilt in the white background of each block. Quilt a leaf pattern through the block backgrounds and in the border.

3. Bind the quilt edges.

4. Add a hanging sleeve and label.

5. Cut the ribbon into ten 3½"-long segments.

6. Set the machine for a feather stitch and thread the needle with the desired decorative thread. Using one ribbon segment for practicing, stitch through the lengthwise center of the ribbon, allowing the stitching to gather up the ribbon. This gives the leaf a realistic "curled" look. Once you are comfortable with stitching on the ribbon, stitch the remaining segments.

7. Trace the small and large leaf patterns on page 52 onto freezer paper. Use the templates to cut a leaf shape from each ribbon segment. If necessary, apply seam sealant to the ribbon edges.

8. Arrange one or two leaves around the stem of each pear. Glue, fuse, or hand stitch the leaves in place.

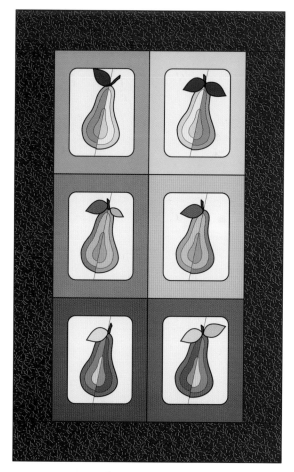

Quilt Assembly Diagram

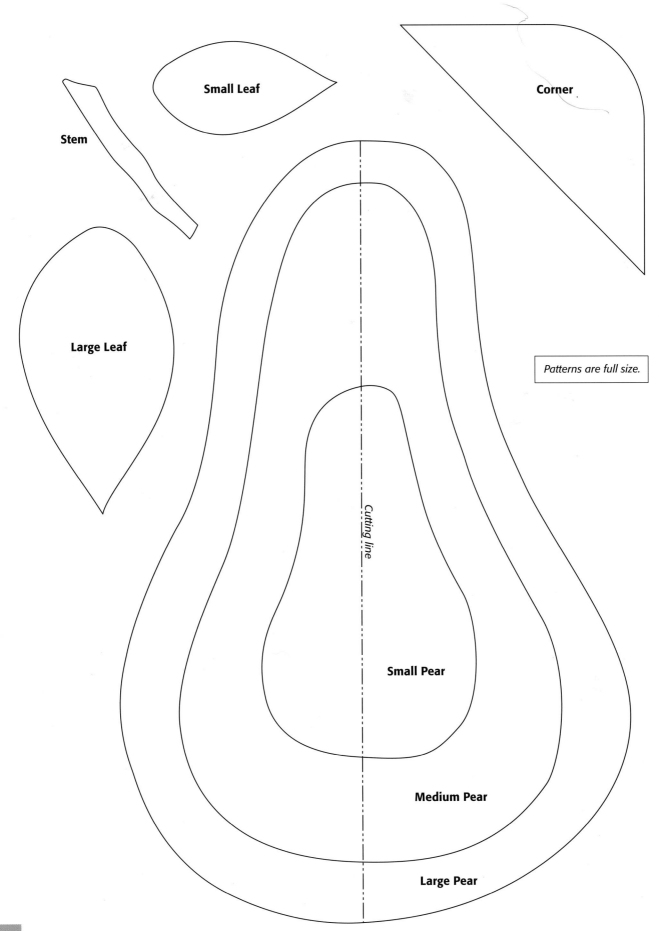

Small Leaf

Corner

Stem

Large Leaf

Patterns are full size.

Cutting line

Small Pear

Medium Pear

Large Pear

DUSTY GULCH

Finished Quilt Size: 49½" x 76½"

Finished Block Size: 7½" x 8"

Pieced by Joan Segna. Machine quilted by Sandy Sims, Heirloom Originals.

In 1976 we built our "cabin in the woods." The site was once part of an old Colorado mining town that is now surrounded by national forests. To this day, there is no running water or electricity; it is truly the "old West." Our daughter says the cabin prepared her for the Peace Corps. Here is a fabric rendition sewn with many happy memories.

—Joan

Materials

Yardage is based on 42"-wide fabric.

- ❖ 30 fat eighths of assorted fabrics for houses and buildings
- ❖ 5" x 11" rectangle *each* of 30 assorted fabrics for doors and windows
- ❖ 1 yard of fabric for outer border
- ❖ ¾ yard *total* of assorted blues for sky
- ❖ ⅝ yard of green for sashing
- ❖ ½ yard of brown for sashing
- ❖ ½ yard of fabric for inner border
- ❖ 1 fat eighth of black for porch frames (optional)
- ❖ 3¼ yards of fabric for backing
- ❖ ⅝ yard of fabric for binding
- ❖ 57" x 84" piece of batting
- ❖ Scraps of lace for window curtains (optional)
- ❖ Scraps of fusible web (optional)
- ❖ 2 sheets, 9" x 12", of inkjet fabric for signs, or 9" x 12" rectangle of a light-color fabric and a permanent black marker
- ❖ Template plastic or heavy cardboard
- ❖ Freezer paper
- ❖ Spray starch

Cutting

All measurements include ¼"-wide seam allowances.

From the assorted blues, cut a *total* of:
22 rectangles, 4" x 5"
8 squares, 3" x 3"

From the brown, cut:
6 strips, 2" x 42"

From the green, cut:
6 strips, 2½" x 42"

From the inner border fabric, cut:
6 strips, 2" x 42"

From the outer border fabric, cut:
6 strips, 5" x 42"

From the backing fabric, cut:
2 pieces, 42" x 57"

From the binding fabric, cut:
7 strips, 2¼" x 42"

Cutting the Houses and Buildings

1. Refer to "Step 1: Make the Templates" on page 11 to make a full-size house pattern, using the house half-pattern on page 58. Trace the full-size house pattern onto template plastic or heavy cardboard and cut it out. Also from the template plastic or heavy cardboard, cut an 8½" x 8½" square for the building front. Trace the curved window pattern, the saloon door patterns, and the steeple and steeple window patterns on pages 58 and 59 onto freezer paper and cut them out. Also from the freezer paper, cut the following

shapes: one 3½" x 4½" rectangle for the door, two 1¼" x 2½" rectangles for the lower windows, and two 1¼" x 1¾" rectangles for the upper windows.

2. Using the house and building templates, trace 22 house shapes and 8 building shapes onto the right side of the fat eighths. Cut out the shapes.

Note: In the quilt on page 53, one house and one building were not split. To make a non-split house, make a full-size house pattern from freezer paper, placing the paper fold along the line for the non-split house rather than along the cutting line. For the non-split building, cut an 8" x 8½" rectangle. Add the doors and windows as instructed but ignore the splitting instructions for these structures.

3. For each house, you will need one door, two lower windows, and either one curved window or two upper windows. Use the templates to cut the shapes for one house from one of the 5" x 11" rectangles; repeat for the remaining houses. Keep the shapes (house, doors, and windows) for each house together and set them aside. If one of the house shapes will be a church, also cut one steeple and one steeple window (optional).

4. For each building, you will need two upper windows, two lower windows, and either one door or two saloon doors. Repeat step 3 with the appropriate templates and the remaining 5" x 11" rectangles.

Making the House and Building Blocks

1. Iron the house, building, window, and door pieces, and the steeple, applying spray starch for stability while sewing. Fold the house, building, door, and curved window shapes in half vertically, right sides together, and lightly press the folds to mark the centers.

2. Select one group of window and door pieces that work well with each house and building. For each house and building with a rectangular door, center the door on the shape, align-

ing the folds and lower edges; pin in place. For buildings with saloon doors, pin the doors ½" from the center fold line, aligning the lower edges. For all of the houses and other buildings, pin a lower window on each side of the door(s), ½" from the sides and ¾" from the top of the door. Pin the upper window(s) in place ¾" above the door on houses and 1" above the door on other buildings. For the curved windows, center the shape ¾" above the door, using the folds as a guide. Position the rectangular upper windows ½" from the house or building center fold line. If one of the houses will be a church, remove the right-side window from the structure.

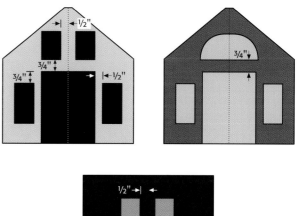

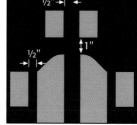

3. Stitch around each door and window ¼" from the edge. Cut away the house or building fabric behind the windows and doors, leaving a ¼" seam allowance. Press each house and building from the wrong side.

4. Using a rotary cutter and ruler, cut each house and building apart on the center fold line. Divide the building halves into two separate piles, one for rectangular doors and one for saloon doors. Divide the house halves into two separate stacks, one for rectangular upper windows and one for curved upper windows. Working from one stack, select a left side for

each right side, making sure the two halves are from different fabrics. Repeat with each of the remaining stacks. When you are satisfied with all of the arrangements, stitch the halves together. Press the seams open.

5. Divide the 22 blue 4" x 5" rectangles into two stacks of 11 rectangles each. Cut each of the rectangles in one stack in half diagonally, cutting from the top left corner to the bottom right corner. These will be stitched to the left side of the house units. Cut each of the rectangles in the remaining stack in half in the opposite direction. These will be stitched to the right side of the house units.

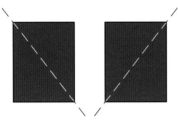

6. With right sides together, place a left-side triangle on the left edge of each house top, positioning the cut edge of the triangles on the diagonal edge of each house unit. Extend the ends slightly beyond the house so the edges will be aligned when stitched; stitch. Press the triangle toward the house corner and the seam toward the triangle. Stitch the right-side triangles to the right edge of each house unit in the same manner. Square up the blocks to 8" x 8½".

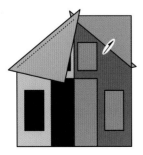

7. If desired, add a blue sky triangle to some or all of the building units. To do so, cut the blue 3" x 3" squares in half diagonally. Position a triangle on the left side of the desired building unit 2¼" from the top left corner as shown. Stitch ¼" from the triangle long edge. Press the triangle toward the building corner. Trim the building corner behind the triangle ¼" from the seam. Repeat for the right side of the building unit.

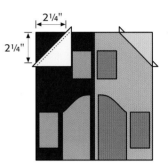

Making the Path Sashing

1. Using a sharp pencil or chalk marker, draw a gently curving line through the lengthwise center of each green strip. With your rotary cutter or scissors, cut each strip apart on the drawn line.

2. With right sides up and the green strips on top, pin a brown strip between each split green strip, leaving approximately ¾" of the brown strip visible as shown. Adjust the strips as necessary so that the units measure 3¼" wide. Stitch along the curved edge of the green strips in each unit, ¼" from the edges. Turn each strip over and trim the excess brown fabric ¼" from the stitching line.

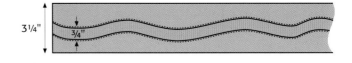

Assembling the Quilt Top

1. Arrange the blocks into six horizontal rows of five blocks each as desired, referring to the quilt assembly diagram if needed. Position a sashing strip at the bottom of each row. When you are satisfied with the house and building arrangement, stitch the blocks in each row together. If you designated one of the house blocks as a church, position the steeple on the right-hand side of the block, aligning the lower edge with the block lower edge and the side of the steeple with the block seam. Stitch the steeple in place ¼" from the top and side edges. Position the window on the steeple, if desired, and stitch it in place.

2. Measure the width of one block row. Trim the sashing strips to the measured length. Stitch a sashing strip to the bottom of each row, and then stitch the rows together. Press the seams toward the sashing rows.

3. Embellish the blocks with porch frames, signs, and curtains, if desired. For the porch frames, cut ⅜"-wide strips of black fabric the length of the top of the door; stitch a strip to each side of the door. Cut one or two more strips to go across the top of the door, referring to the photo on page 53 for guidance; stitch them in place.

   To create signs for the building fronts, use your computer printer or hand write the names. If you print the names on fabric using your computer printer, follow the inkjet fabric manufacturer's instructions. If you hand write the names, cut the signs from the light-color fat quarter and print the desired store name on the strip. The finished signs should measure 1" x 3½". Pin the signs to the top of the desired doorways and then fuse them in place or stitch ⅛" from the edges.

   For curtains, cut small pieces of lace and fuse or hand stitch them to the windows.

4. Measure the quilt top for borders as instructed in "Step 8: Add the Borders" on page 13. Piece and cut the inner side border strips to the required length and stitch them to the quilt sides. Piece and cut the inner top and bottom border strips and stitch them to the top and bottom edges of the quilt top. Repeat with the outer border strips, piecing and cutting as necessary to achieve the required length.

Finishing

Refer to "Finishing Your Quilt" on pages 15–17.

1. Layer the quilt top with batting and backing; baste.

2. Quilt around the houses, doors, and windows. Meander stitch through the sky portions of the blocks. Add texture to the houses by stitching vertical and horizontal rows that resemble wood siding. Randomly stitch grass-like tufts through the sashing.

3. Bind the quilt edges.

4. Add a hanging sleeve and label.

Quilt Assembly Diagram

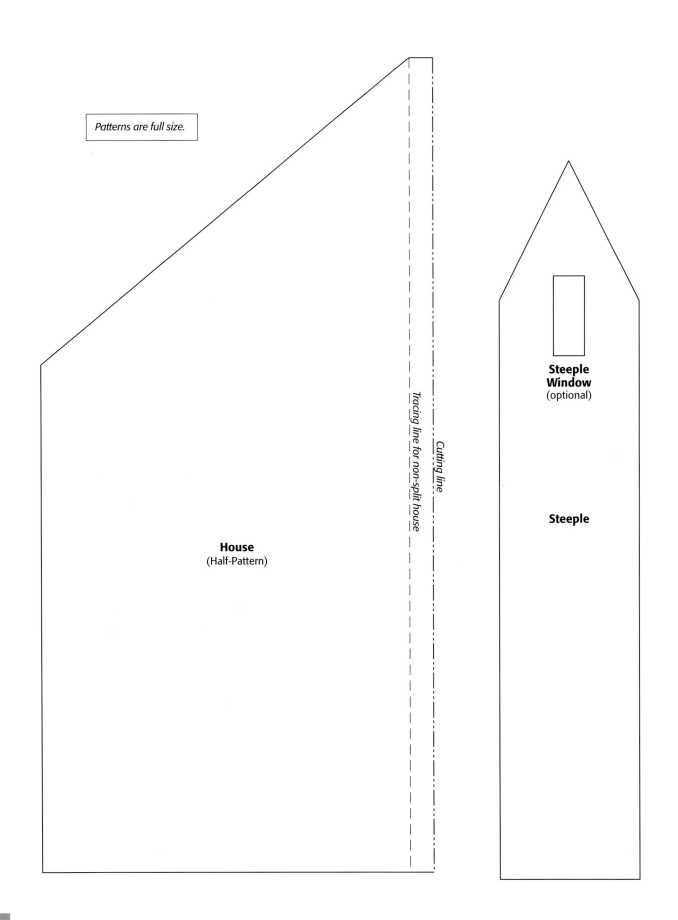

Patterns are full size.

Tracing line for non-split house

Cutting line

House
(Half-Pattern)

**Steeple
Window**
(optional)

Steeple

Patterns are full size.

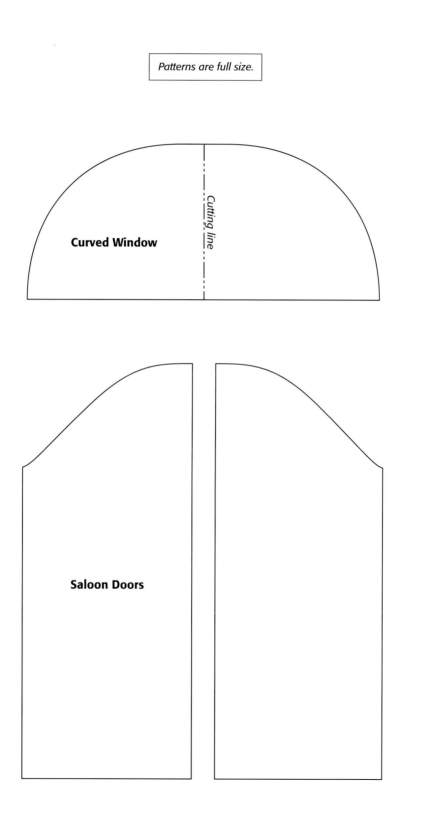

Curved Window

Cutting line

Saloon Doors

Finished Quilt Size: 19⅝" x 61"

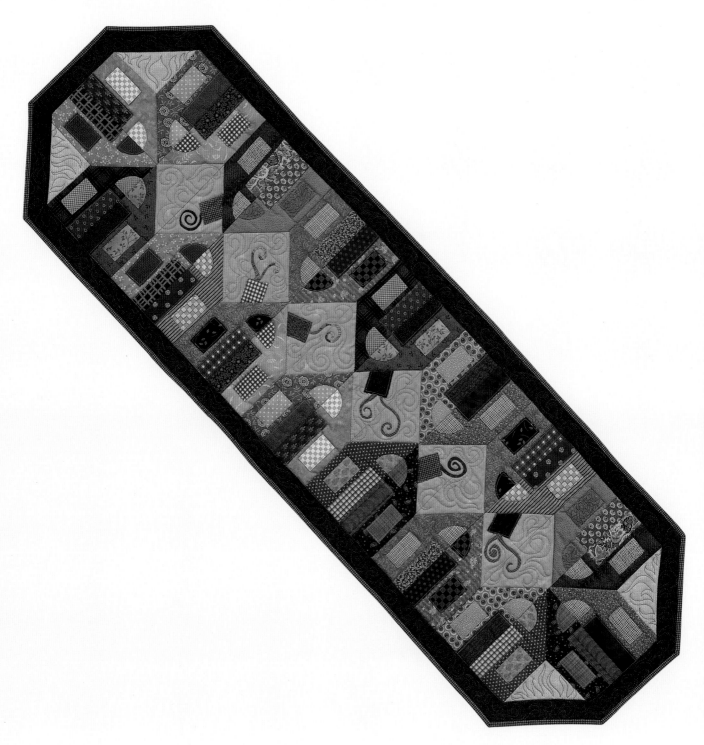

Pieced by Jayme Crow. Machine quilted by Sandy Sims, Heirloom Originals.

There is such a sense of community when you live in a place where small row houses snuggle around a common area and everything is within walking distance.

Materials

Yardage is based on 42"-wide fabric.

- ❖ 16 fat eighths of assorted fabrics for houses
- ❖ ½ yard of brown for border
- ❖ 4" x 6" rectangle *each* of 16 different fabrics that coordinate with house fabrics for windows
- ❖ 4" x 6" rectangle *each* of 16 different fabrics that coordinate with house fabrics for doors
- ❖ 1 fat quarter of blue for sky
- ❖ 4" x 6" rectangle of 3 different grayish-tan prints for smoke swirls
- ❖ 6" x 11" rectangle of green for grass
- ❖ 3" x 3" square *each* of 6 different browns for chimneys
- ❖ 2 yards of fabric for backing
- ❖ ⅜ yard of fabric for binding
- ❖ 25" x 65" piece of batting
- ❖ 9" x 12" rectangle of paper-backed fusible web
- ❖ Freezer paper
- ❖ Spray starch

Cutting

All measurements include ¼"-wide seam allowances.

From the blue, cut:
3 squares, 8⅞" x 8⅞"; cut each square in half twice diagonally to yield 12 quarter-square triangles

From the green, cut:
1 square, 8" x 8"; cut the square in half twice diagonally to yield 4 quarter-square triangles

From the brown for the border, cut:
5 strips, 2¼" x 42"

From the binding fabric, cut:
4 strips, 2¼" x 42"

From the backing fabric, cut:
1 piece, 25" x 65"

Cutting the House Pieces

1. Refer to "Step 1: Make the Templates" on page 11 to make a full-size house pattern, using the house half-pattern on page 64. Trace the full-size house pattern and the curved window pattern on page 64 onto freezer paper and cut them out. Also from the freezer paper, cut the following shapes: one 3½" x 4½" rectangle for the door, two 1¼" x 2⅜" rectangles for the lower windows, and one 1½" x 2⅜" rectangle for the chimney.

2. Use the house template to cut one shape from each of the 16 fat eighths. From each 4" x 6" window rectangle, cut two lower windows and one curved window, using the appropriate templates. Keep the windows from each rectangle together. In the same manner, use the door template to cut one door from each of the 4" x 6" door rectangles and one chimney from each of the six brown squares.

Making the Houses

1. Iron the house, window, and door pieces, applying spray starch for stability while sewing. Fold the house, door, and curved window shapes in half vertically, right sides together, and lightly press the folds to mark the centers.

2. Select one group of windows and a door that work well with each house. For each house, center the door on the house, aligning the center folds and lower edges; pin in place. Center the curved window ½" above the door, using the fold lines as a guide; pin in place. Pin a lower window in place ¼" from each side of the door and ¾" from the top of the door. Stitch ⅛" from the raw edges of each window and the sides and top of each door. Cut away the house fabric behind the windows and doors, leaving a ¼" seam allowance. Press each house from the wrong side.

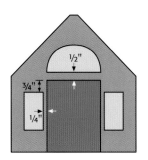

3. With a rotary cutter and ruler, cut each house in half vertically, using the fold line as a guide. Pair each left half with a different right half. When you are satisfied with the pairings, stitch the halves together. Press the seams open.

Assembling the Table Runner Top

1. Refer to the table runner assembly diagram to arrange the houses into two rows of seven houses each, positioning the houses so that they are point to point. Place the remaining two houses at each end. Place the sky triangles in the open areas between the houses so that the triangles' straight-grain edge is aligned with the sides of the house. Place the grass triangles along the sides of each end house so the straight-grain edge will be along the outside edge of the table runner. Position each chimney on the sky piece above the desired rooftop.

2. One at a time, remove the sky triangles with chimneys. Align the bottom of the chimney with the triangle edge; straight stitch the chimneys in place ⅛" from the side and top edges. Turn the triangle to the wrong side and cut away the sky fabric behind the chimney, leaving a ¼" seam allowance.

3. Stitch each end house and the two houses adjacent to it together as shown with the sky triangle. Inset the grass triangles into the openings.

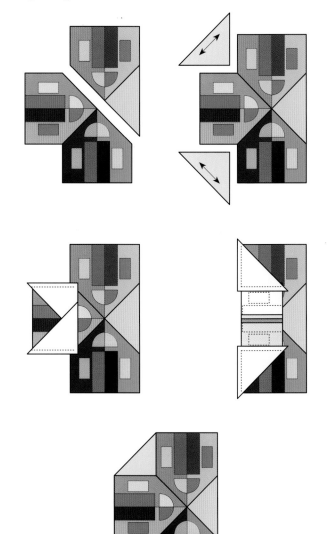

4. Stitch the remaining houses and sky triangles together in pairs as shown.

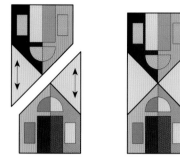

5. Stitch the pairs together and then stitch the end pieces to each end of the center house strip.

6. Follow the manufacturer's instructions to trace each of the smoke swirl patterns on page 64 onto the paper side of the fusible web two times. Cut out the swirls ⅛" from the lines. Fuse two different swirls to the wrong side of each 4" x 6" smoke swirl rectangle. Cut out the swirls on the traced lines and remove the paper backing. Position each swirl on the table runner above a chimney and fuse it in place.

7. Refer to "Step 8: Add the Borders" on page 13 to stitch two border strips together to make one long piece, using a bias seam. Measure one long side of the table runner. Cut the pieced border strip approximately 2" longer than the length measured. Stitch the strip to the side of the table runner, extending the strip about 1" at each end. Trim the ends even with the angled sides of the table runner as shown. Repeat with the remaining side. Cut and stitch border strips to the four angled sides and then add the end borders to the table runner in the same manner.

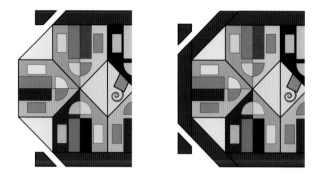

Finishing
Refer to "Finishing Your Quilt" on pages 15–17.

1. Layer the table runner top with backing and batting; baste.
2. Quilt in the ditch around the houses, windows, and doors. Quilt a swirl design in the sky area and a grass motif in the grass triangles. Use a decorative design to quilt the border.
3. Bind the table runner edges.
4. Add a label.

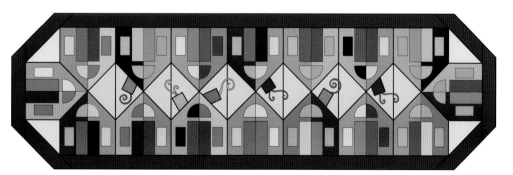

Table Runner Assembly Diagram

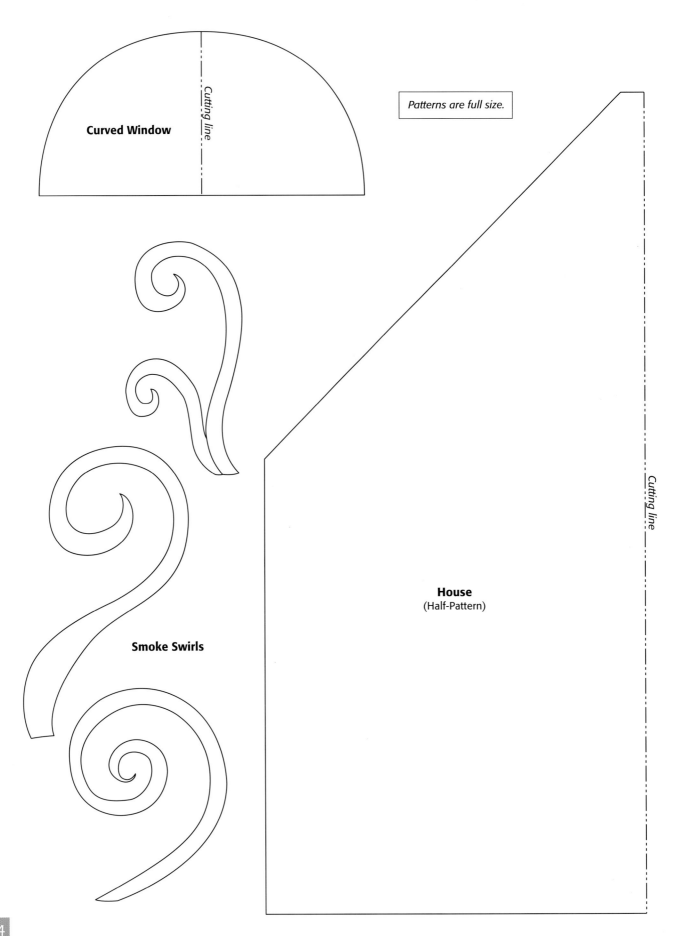

Curved Window

Cutting line

Patterns are full size.

Cutting line

Smoke Swirls

House
(Half-Pattern)

Finished Quilt Size: 35" x 48"

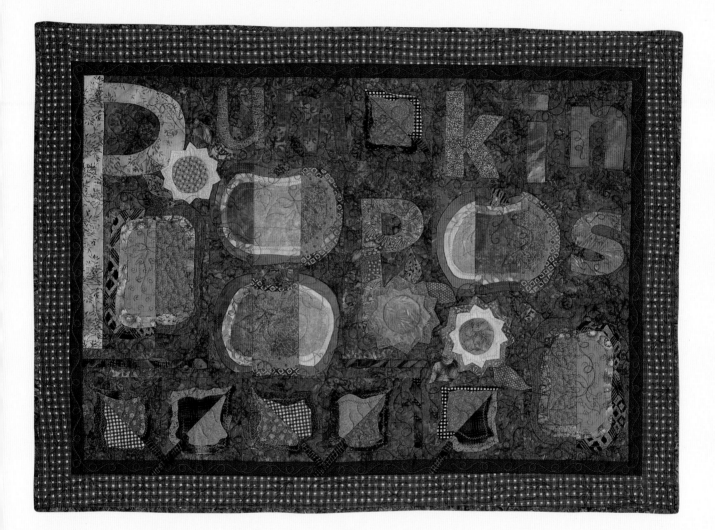

Pieced by Jerrine Kirsch. Machine quilted by Sandy Sims, Heirloom Originals.

Autumn is such a treat for the senses! Feel the crispness in the air, see the blazing colors, and taste the bounty fall brings as you enjoy this seasonal wall hanging.

Materials

Yardage is based on 42"-wide fabric.

❖ 1½ yards of green for block backgrounds

❖ ⅝ yard of fabric for outer border

❖ 1 fat eighth *each* of 5 different dark, 5 different medium, and 5 different light fabrics from the orange family for pumpkins and letters

❖ 10" x 10" square *each* of 12 different fabrics from the green family for leaves

❖ 1 fat eighth *each* of 9 different fabrics from the yellow family for letters and sunflowers

❖ ¼ yard of fabric for inner border

❖ 1 fat eighth of dark brown for vine trellis

❖ Scraps of assorted medium browns for pumpkin and leaf stems

❖ 1¾ yards of fabric for backing

❖ ½ yard of fabric for binding

❖ 42" x 54" piece of batting

❖ ¾ yard of 18"-wide paper-backed fusible web

❖ 1½ yards of ½"-wide green double-faced satin ribbon for vine

❖ Freezer paper

❖ Spray starch

Cutting

All measurements include ¼"-wide seam allowances.

From the green, cut*:
2 rectangles, 9" x 14" (blocks 8 and 20)
3 rectangles, 9" x 11½" (blocks 9, 11, and 13)
1 square, 8½" x 8½" (block 1)
1 rectangle, 6½" x 7½" (block 14)
1 rectangle, 7" x 14½" (block 10)
6 squares, 7" x 7" (blocks 4 and 15–19)
1 rectangle, 6½" x 8½" (block 5)
1 square, 6½" x 6½" (block 3)
2 rectangles, 5½" x 8½" (blocks 7 and 12)
1 rectangle, 5" x 6½" (block 2)
1 rectangle, 4½" x 8½" (block 6)
1 rectangle, 2½" x 10½" (strip A)
1 rectangle, 2½" x 7" (strip B)
1 rectangle, 2½" x 6½" (strip C)
1 rectangle, 1½" x 6½" (strip D)
*Mark the block number or strip letter on each piece as it is cut for ease in identifying later.

From the dark brown, cut:
3 strips, 1½" x 22"

From the inner border fabric, cut:
4 strips, 1½" x 42"

From the outer border fabric, cut:
5 strips, 3" x 42"

From the backing fabric, cut:
1 piece, 42" x 54"

From the binding fabric, cut:
5 strips, 2¼" x 42"

Cutting the Pumpkins, Flowers, Leaves, and Letters

1. Enlarge the small, medium, and large tall and short pumpkin patterns on pages 71 and 72 by the percentage indicated. Trace each of the enlarged pumpkin patterns onto freezer paper and cut them out. Trace the large and small flower patterns on page 73 and the large and small split leaves on page 74 onto freezer paper and cut them out.

2. Use the short pumpkin templates to cut one large pumpkin from each of three dark orange fat eighths, one medium pumpkin from each of three medium orange fat eighths, and one small pumpkin from each of three light orange fat eighths.

3. Use the tall pumpkin templates to cut one large pumpkin from each of the two remaining dark orange fat eighths, one medium pumpkin from each of the two remaining medium orange fat eighths, and one small pumpkin from each of the two remaining light orange fat eighths.

4. Cut two large flowers and three small flowers from different yellow fabrics, using the appropriate templates.

5. Cut one large split leaf each from six different green squares and one small split leaf each from the remaining six green squares, using the appropriate templates.

6. Follow the manufacturer's instructions to trace the following number of shapes onto the paper side of the fusible web: flower center on page 73 three times; leaves A, B, and C on page 73 two times each; the letters on pages 74–77 one time each; three short pumpkin stems, and two tall pumpkin stems. Cut out the shapes approximately ⅛" from the lines. Fuse each flower center shape to the wrong side of a different yellow fabric and each leaf to the wrong side of the remainder of the green squares. Fuse the curved portion of the P to the wrong side of

the remaining yellow fat eighth; cut one 2" x 20½" strip from the remainder of the fat eighth for the P stem. Fuse the remaining letters to the wrong sides of any of the remaining fabric from the orange and yellow fat eighths, and the pumpkin stems to the brown scraps. Cut out the shapes on the drawn lines. *Do not remove the paper backing until you are ready to apply the shape to the background fabric.*

Making the Blocks

1. Iron the tall pumpkins, short pumpkins, large and small split leaves, and large and small flower shapes, applying spray starch for stability while sewing. Fold the shapes in half vertically, right sides together, and lightly press the folds to mark the centers. Repeat to mark the centers of background rectangles 8, 9, 11, 13, and 20, referring to the block diagram on page 69 for the vertical length. Fold the background squares for blocks 4 and 15–19 in half diagonally, right sides together, and press the folds lightly to mark the centers.

2. For each of the two tall pumpkin units, select a large, medium, and small pumpkin shape that work well together. Measure 1½" from the bottom of block background rectangles 8 and 20 and lightly mark a dot on the fold lines with a sharp pencil. Center the large tall pumpkin from each unit on a background rectangle, aligning the bottom of the pumpkin with the marked dot and using the folds as a guide; pin in place. Stitch around each pumpkin, ¼" from the raw edge. Cut away the background fabric behind each large pumpkin appliqué, leaving a ¼" seam allowance. Center the medium pumpkin from each unit over the large pumpkin. Stitch ¼" from the raw edge, and then cut away the large pumpkin fabric behind each medium pumpkin appliqué as before. Center the small pumpkin from each unit over the medium pumpkin; cut away the

medium pumpkin fabric behind each small pumpkin appliqué. Press the units from the wrong side.

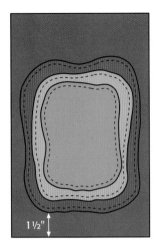

3. Cut each appliquéd pumpkin rectangle in half, following the fold lines.
4. Stitch the right half from one unit to the left half of the other unit and vise versa. Press the seams open. Square up each block to 8½" x 12½", keeping the pumpkins centered.

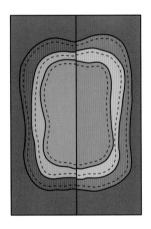

5. For each of the three short pumpkin units, select a large, medium, and small pumpkin shape that work well together. Measure ¾" from the bottom of block background rectangles 9, 11, and 13 and lightly mark a dot on the fold lines with a sharp pencil. Refer to step 2 to stitch the large, medium, and small pumpkin shapes to the rectangle, cutting away the

fabric behind the appliqué after each addition. Press the units from the wrong side.

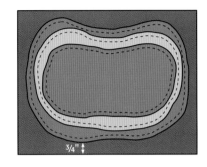

6. Refer to the pattern to cut each rectangle into thirds along the suggested cutting lines.
7. Select a different left, middle, and right third from each unit. When you are satisfied with all of the arrangements, stitch the thirds together. Press the seams open. Square up each block to 10½" x 8½", keeping the pumpkin centered.

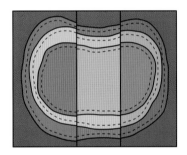

8. Fuse the appropriate stem to the center top of each pumpkin, following the manufacturer's instructions. Stitch around the outside of each stem with a decorative stitch.
9. For each of the six leaf units, select one large and one small leaf shape that work well together. Refer to step 2 to center the large and small leaf shapes diagonally on background squares 4 and 15–19, stitching them in place ¼" from the raw edges and trimming away the fabric behind the appliqué after each addition. Press the units from the wrong side.

10. Cut each leaf unit in half diagonally, following the fold lines.

11. Select a different right half for each left half. When you are satisfied with all of the arrangements, stitch the halves together. Press the seams open. Square up each block to 6½" x 6½".

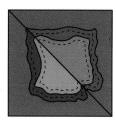

12. Refer to the manufacturer's instructions and the quilt diagram below to fuse the appropriate letter to each background rectangle. Fuse the curved portion of the P to the block 1 background square. Zigzag or blanket stitch around the edges of each letter.

Making the Vine Strips and Leaf Stems

1. Fold each dark brown 1½" x 22" strip in half lengthwise, right sides together. Stitch ¼" from the long, raw edges. Turn the strip to the right side; press.

2. From the strips, cut one 10½" length, one 7" length, and one 6½" length for the vines. Cut three 2½" lengths and three 4" lengths for the leaf stems.

3. Center the 10½" length on strip A, the 7" length on strip B, and the 6½" length on strip C. Stitch across each strip at 1" intervals as shown.

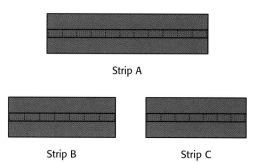

Strip A

Strip B   Strip C

4. Hand or machine appliqué a 2½" stem in place at the base of three leaf blocks. Set the remaining stems aside. They will be applied after the borders have been attached.

Assembling the Quilt Top

1. Arrange the blocks and yellow 2" x 20½" strip into units as shown. Stitch the blocks in each unit together and then stitch the units together.

2" x 20½"

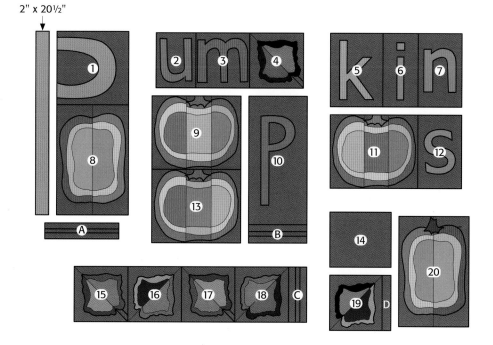

2. Measure the quilt top for borders as instructed in "Step 8: Add the Borders" on page 13. Cut the inner side border strips to the required length and stitch them to the quilt sides. Piece and cut the top and bottom inner border strips to the required length and stitch them to the top and bottom edges of the quilt top. Repeat with the outer border strips, piecing and cutting the strips as needed to achieve the required length.

3. Select a small flower shape and flower center that work well together. Refer to the quilt assembly diagram below and the photo on page 65 to position the small flower shape only between blocks 1 and 9. For the remaining two flower units, select one large flower, one small flower, and one flower center that work well together. Position the large flower shape from one unit on block 10 and the remaining large flower shape on block 14. Tuck two A, B, or C leaves under each flower shape as desired. Remove the flowers and fuse the leaves in place, following the manufacturer's instructions.

4. Reposition the small flower between blocks 1 and 9. Stitch around the flower, ¼" from the raw edges. Cut away the fabric behind the flower appliqué, leaving a ¼" seam allowance. Reposition the large flower on block 10. Stitch around the flower ¼" from the raw edges. Cut away the fabric behind the appliqué as before. Position the small flower over the large flower. Stitch ¼" from the raw edge, and then cut away the large flower fabric behind the small flower appliqué. Repeat to stitch the large and small flower shapes to block 14. Position a flower center on each flower; fuse it in place. Zigzag or blanket stitch around the edges of each center shape.

5. Position a 4"-long stem on each of the remaining leaf blocks. Extend the stems into the border and trim them to the desired length. Hand or machine appliqué the stems in place.

Finishing
Refer to "Finishing Your Quilt" on pages 15–17.

1. Layer the quilt top with backing and batting; baste.
2. Quilt ¼" from the pumpkin and flower shapes, following the previous stitching. Quilt a swirl in the flower centers to add texture. Quilt the entire top with an overall pattern of vines and leaves, going through all of the shapes.
3. Weave the ribbon through the openings created by the stitching on the A, B, and C strips to create a vine look. Hand tack the ribbon ends to secure.
4. Bind the quilt edges.
5. Add a hanging sleeve and label.

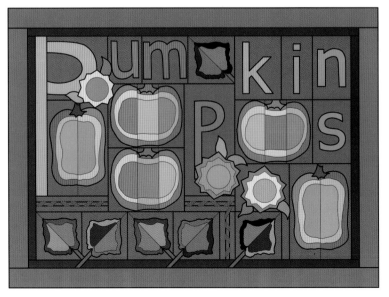

Quilt Assembly Diagram

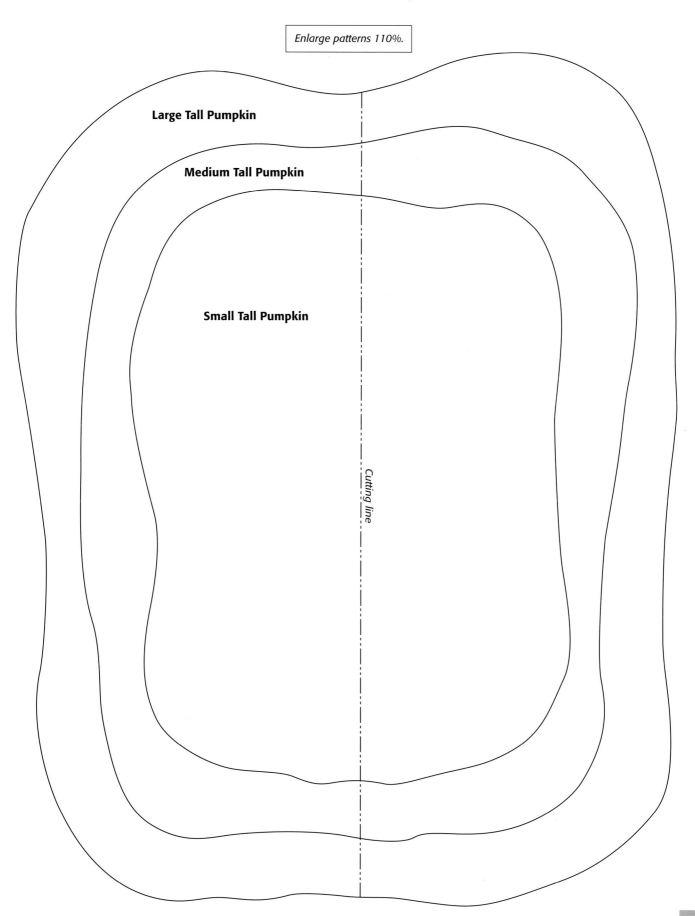

Enlarge patterns 110%.

Large Tall Pumpkin

Medium Tall Pumpkin

Small Tall Pumpkin

Cutting line

Enlarge patterns 110%.

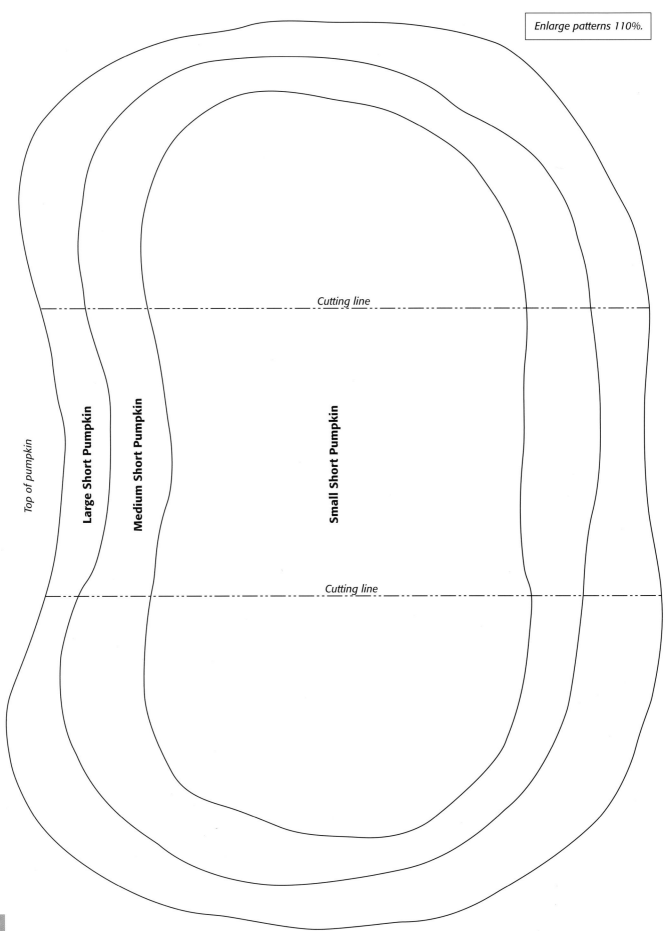

Cutting line

Top of pumpkin

Large Short Pumpkin

Medium Short Pumpkin

Small Short Pumpkin

Cutting line

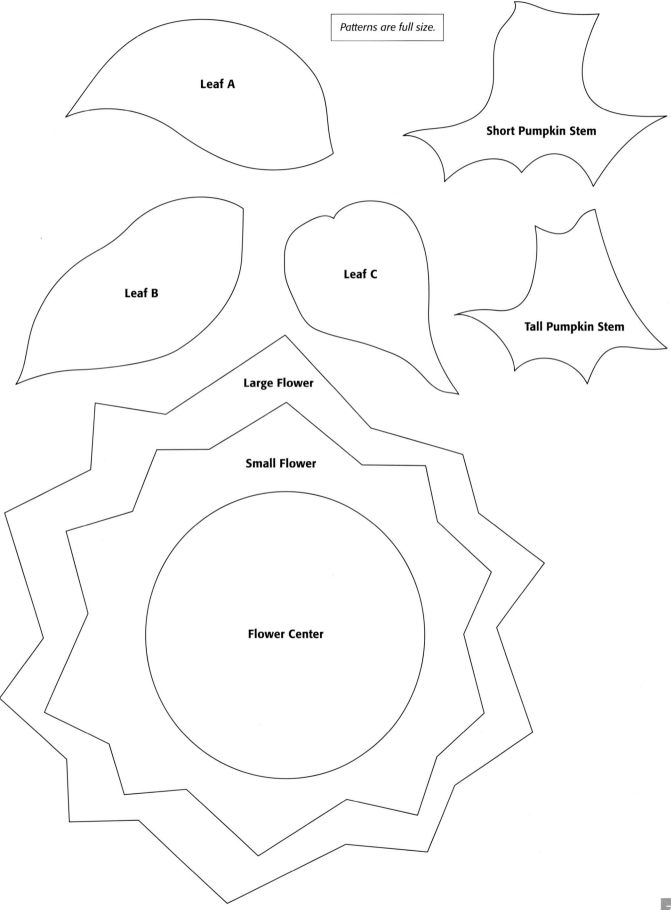

Leaf A

Patterns are full size.

Short Pumpkin Stem

Leaf B

Leaf C

Tall Pumpkin Stem

Large Flower

Small Flower

Flower Center

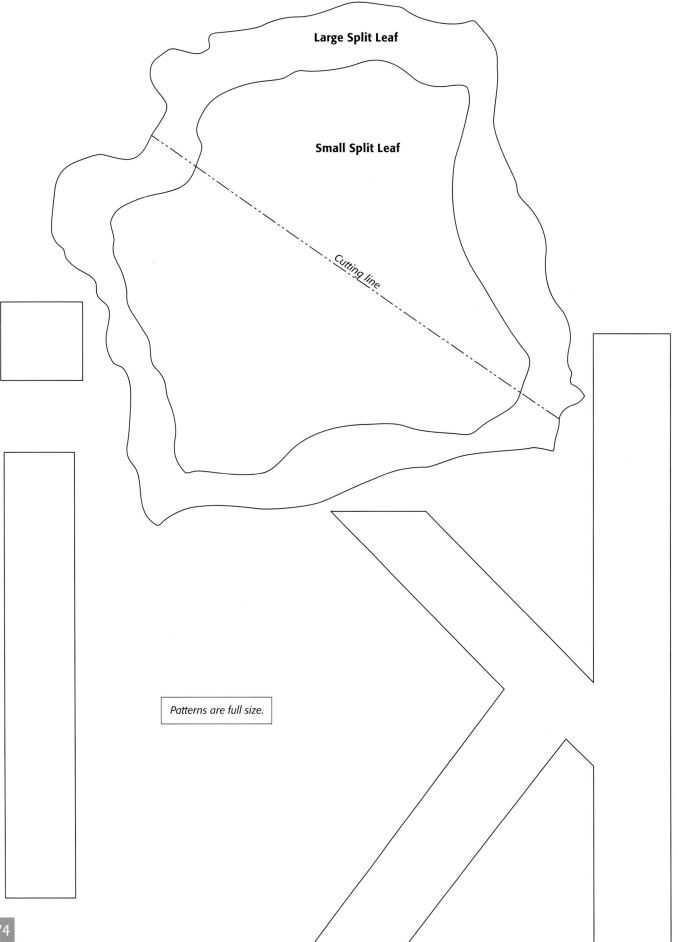

Large Split Leaf

Small Split Leaf

Cutting line

Patterns are full size.

Pattern is full size.

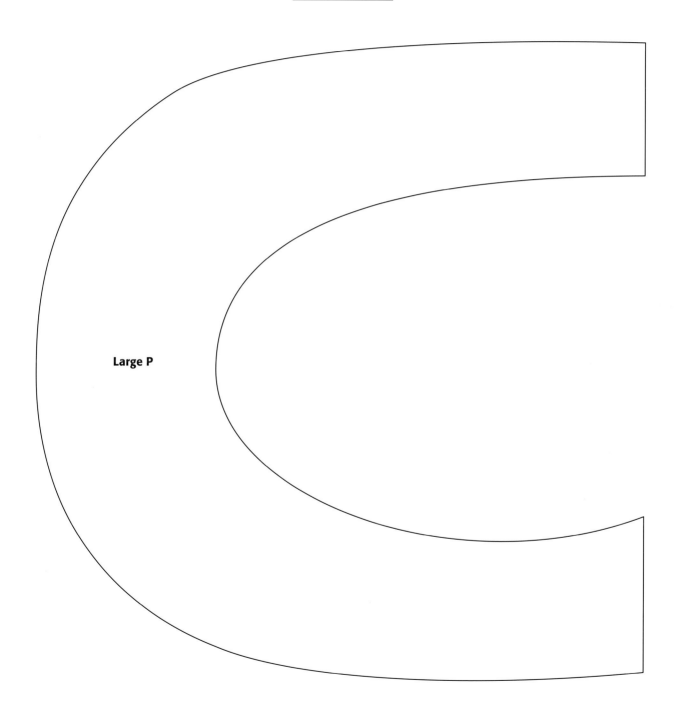

Large P

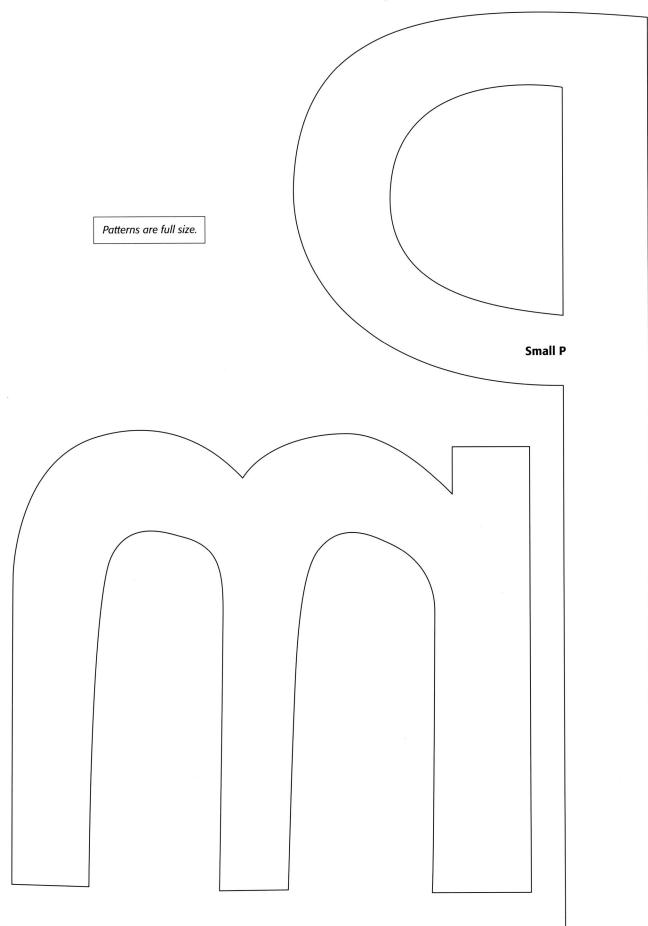

Patterns are full size.

Small P

Patterns are full size.

LEAVES ALONG THE PATH

Finished Quilt Size: 19" x 47"

Pieced by Joan Segna and Jayme Crow.
Machine quilted by Sandy Sims, Heirloom Originals.

The riot of gold, orange, and rust trees signal that fall is here. Leaves flutter from the trees and settle onto the path, creating a wonderful pattern at our feet.

Materials

Yardage is based on 42"-wide fabric.

- ❖ 1⅜ yards of gold for background

- ❖ 10" x 10" square *each* of 4 different fall-color fabrics for large leaves

- ❖ 8" x 8" square *each* of 4 different fall-color fabrics for medium leaves

- ❖ 5" x 5" square *each* of 13 different fall-color fabrics for small leaves

- ❖ 30 squares, 3½" x 3½", of assorted batiks for pebbles

- ❖ ¼ yard of fabric for inner border

- ❖ ⅜ yard of fabric for outer border

- ❖ 1¾ yards of fabric for backing

- ❖ ⅜ yard of fabric for binding

- ❖ 25" x 53" piece of batting

- ❖ Decorative threads for embellishing

- ❖ ⅝ yard of 22"-wide paper-backed fusible web

- ❖ Freezer paper

- ❖ Spray starch

Cutting

All measurements include ¼"-wide seam allowances.

From the gold, cut:
1 piece, 14" x 42"

From the inner border fabric, cut:
3 strips, 1" x 42"

From the outer border fabric, cut:
4 strips, 2½" x 42"

From the fusible web, cut:
30 squares, 3½" x 3½"

From the backing fabric, cut:
1 piece, 25" x 53"

From the binding fabric, cut:
4 strips, 2¼" x 42"

Assembling the Quilt Top

1. Press the background piece. Fold the piece in half lengthwise and gently press the fold to mark the center.

2. On the background piece wrong side, measure 5½" from the corner toward the center of the short edge as shown on page 80 and make a mark with a sharp pencil. Measure 6½" from the same corner along the long edge and make

a mark. Draw a line to connect the marks. Repeat at the opposite end.

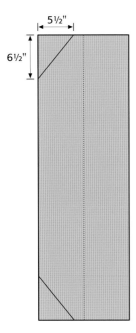

3. Fold the background piece in half along the fold line. Pin the raw edges together between the marked lines. Using your rotary cutter and ruler, cut along the lines through both thicknesses.

4. Measure the two long side edges and cut two inner border strips 2" longer than the length measured. Stitch the strips to each long side of the background piece, allowing the strip ends to extend 1" beyond the ends of the background. Press the seams toward the borders. Trim the ends even with the angled edges. Repeat to cut and stitch the angled side borders, trimming the excess even with the sides and end, and then the end borders, trimming the excess even with the angled sides.

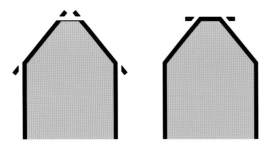

5. Repeat step 4 with the outer border strips.

Cutting and Applying the Pebbles

1. Follow the manufacturer's instructions to trace one pebble shape onto the paper side of each fusible-web square, using the patterns on page 83. Trace an additional pebble onto 10 of the squares for a total of 40 pebble shapes. Fuse each fusible-web square to the wrong side of a pebble-fabric square. Cut out the pebbles on the traced lines. Remove the paper backing.

2. Refer to the table runner assembly diagram on page 81 to arrange the pebbles through the center of the background piece. The pebbles should be spaced about ⅛" apart, as if mortar were between them. If needed, reshape the pebbles so they fit together nicely. When you are satisfied with the arrangement, fuse the pebbles in place, following the manufacturer's instructions.

Quilting the Table Runner
Refer to "Finishing Your Quilt" on pages 15-17.

1. Layer the table runner top with backing and batting; baste.

2. Quilt around each pebble. Quilt pebble shapes throughout the background. Quilt in the ditch between the background and inner border seams and between the inner and outer border seams. Use a decorative stitch to quilt the outer border.

Cutting and Applying the Leaves

1. Enlarge the leaf templates on page 82 by the percentage indicated. Trace the enlarged leaves onto freezer paper and cut them out.

2. Use the large leaf template to cut one shape from each of the four large-leaf fabrics. Cut four medium leaves and 13 small leaves, using the appropriate templates and fabrics.

3. Iron the leaf shapes, applying spray starch for stability while sewing. Fold the large and medium leaves and four of the small leaves in half vertically and lightly press the folds to mark the centers.

4. For each of the four leaf units, select one large, one medium, and one small rust leaf shape. Center the medium leaf from each unit on the large leaf, using the folds as a guide; pin in place. Stitch around each medium leaf, ⅛" from the raw edge. Cut away the large leaf fabric behind the medium leaf, leaving a ¼" seam allowance. Press the unit from the wrong side.

5. With your rotary cutter and ruler, cut the leaf units into four pieces, following the suggested cutting lines on the pattern.

6. Arrange pieces from four different leaf units to form each new leaf. When you are satisfied with all of the arrangements, stitch the pieces together. Press the seams open.

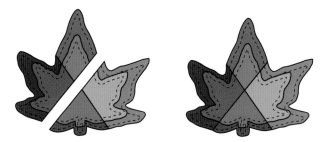

7. Center the small leaf appliqué on each leaf unit, using the folds as a guide; pin in place. Stitch ⅛" from the raw edges of each small leaf. *Do not cut away the fabric behind the small leaf.*

Finishing

1. Arrange the four leaf units on the table runner top, referring to the table runner assembly diagram below; pin in place. Position the nine individual small leaves on the top as desired. When you are satisfied with the arrangement, stitch the leaf units in place ¼" from the edges of the large leaf appliqué. Using decorative thread, stitch a vein pattern through each small leaf, including those on the leaf units.

2. Refer to "Binding" on page 15 to bind the table runner edges.

3. Add a label.

Table Runner Assembly Diagram

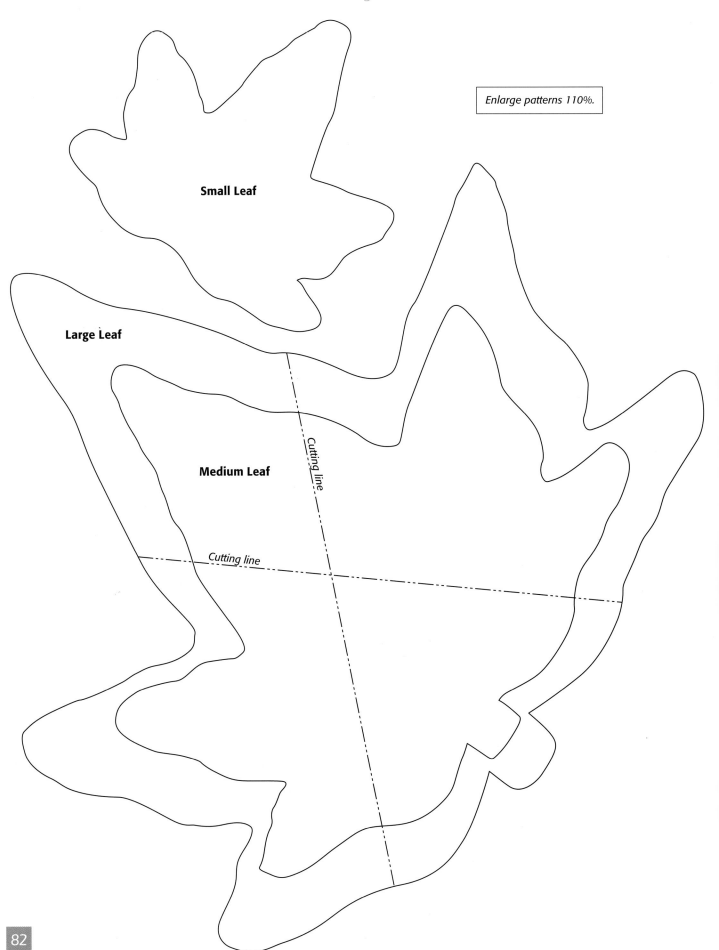

Enlarge patterns 110%.

Small Leaf

Large Leaf

Medium Leaf

Cutting line

Cutting line

Pebbles

Patterns are full size.

STARRY NIGHT PINES

Finished Quilt Size: 29" x 51"

Pieced and machine quilted by Joan Segna.

In this wintry scene, snowflakes fall gently from the night sky to paint the landscape with a fresh new coat of white.

Materials

Yardage is based on 42"-wide fabric.

- ❖ 1 fat quarter *each* of white, light blue, dark blue, and green for trees
- ❖ ⅞ yard of black snowflake print for sky and inner border
- ❖ ¾ yard of icy blue for mountain
- ❖ ½ yard of white for snow
- ❖ ⅜ yard of dark blue for sky
- ❖ ⅜ yard of fabric for outer border
- ❖ 8" x 8" square of brown for tree trunks
- ❖ 1⅞ yards of fabric for backing
- ❖ ½ yard of fabric for binding
- ❖ 35" x 57" piece of batting
- ❖ Clear monofilament thread
- ❖ 9" x 12" rectangle of paper-backed fusible web
- ❖ Chalk marker
- ❖ Assorted beads for embellishing trees
- ❖ Paper for making patterns

Cutting

All measurements include ¼"-wide seam allowances.

From the snowflake print, cut:
5 strips, 2" x 42"
2 strips, 5" x 42"
3 strips, 1¾" x 42"

From the dark blue, cut:
5 strips, 2" x 42"

From the icy blue, cut:
1 piece, 19" x 40"

From the white, cut:
1 piece, 11" x 40"

From the outer border fabric, cut:
4 strips, 2¼" x 42"

From the backing fabric, cut:
1 piece, 35" x 57"

From the binding fabric, cut:
5 strips, 2¼" x 42"

Making the Background

1. Alternately stitch the dark blue and snowflake print 2" x 42" strips together along the long edges as shown to make a strip set. Press the seams in one direction. From the strip set, crosscut 20 segments, 2" wide.

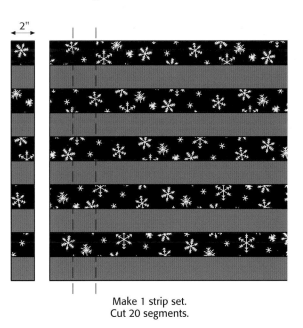

Make 1 strip set.
Cut 20 segments.

2. Stitch 18 segments together, reversing every other segment as shown on page 86. Beginning with a blue square, count down five squares from the top of one of the remaining segments and unsew the seam. Stitch the two five-square segments together as shown on page 86 and then stitch the unit to the larger

piece, aligning the upper edges. Count down four squares from the top of the remaining segment and unsew the seam. Count down another four squares and unsew that seam as well. Stitch the two four-square segments together as shown and then stitch the unit to the larger piece, aligning the upper edges. Stitch the two-square segment to the larger piece as shown. Press.

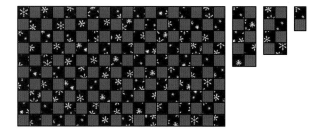

3. On a large sheet of paper, draw a 39" x 22½" rectangle. Place the checkerboard piece on the left side of the rectangle, aligning the top and left edges. Lightly trace around the bottom and right sides. Remove the piece. Beginning at the left of the stair-stepped edge on the paper, draw a gently curved slope for the mountain, referring to the photo on page 84 as necessary. The line must be drawn at least ½" inside the previous line. Using the measurements shown, draw another gently curving line at the bottom of the paper rectangle for the snow. Cut the paper rectangle apart on the curved lines.

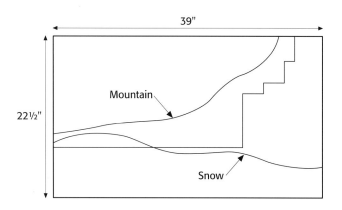

4. Pin the mountain pattern to the right side of the mountain fabric and cut it out, adding ¼" to all of the curved edges for seam allowance. Press under the curved edges ¼". Pin the snow pattern to the right side of the snow fabric and cut it out, adding ¼" to the upper curved edge. Press under the curved upper edge ¼".

Assembling the Quilt Top

1. Layer the backing and batting as described in "Layering and Basting" on page 15.

2. Pin the checkerboard piece, right side up, to the batting 6" from the top and bottom edges of the batting and 9" from the sides of the batting. Pin the mountain piece to the checkerboard piece, placing the curved edge over the staggered edge of the checkerboard piece until the upper edge measures 39". Be sure the sides remain aligned. Pin the snow piece to the bottom of the mountain piece, overlapping the edges until the sides measure 22½".

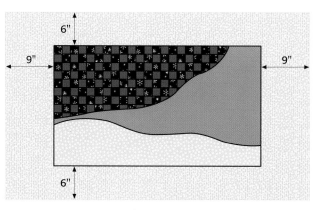

3. Thread the machine with monofilament in the needle and all-purpose thread that matches the background in the bobbin. Set up the machine for a blind hem stitch. Carefully stitch along the pressed-under edges of the mountain and snow pieces.

4. Set up the machine for quilting. Quilt in the ditch of the checkerboard seams. Quilt contour lines on the mountain piece and rows of gently curving lines on the snow piece.

Making and Applying the Trees

1. Enlarge the large tree pattern on page 90 by the percentage indicated. Trace the enlarged large tree onto freezer paper and cut it out.

2. Using the pattern, cut one large tree from each of the four fat quarters. Iron each tree, applying spray starch for stability while sewing. Fold the shapes in half vertically, right sides together, and lightly press the folds to mark the centers. Using scissors, cut each tree vertically into four pieces, following the suggested cutting lines on the pattern.

3. Arrange one piece from each of the four trees to form each new tree. When you are satisfied with the arrangements, pin the pieces together and set them aside.

4. Trace one of each of the three small trees on page 89 onto the paper side of the fusible web, following the manufacturer's instruction. Also trace the tree trunk on page 89 onto the fusible web four times. Cut out each shape ⅛" from the lines. Fuse each tree to the wrong side of the remainder of different large tree fat quarters. Fuse the tree trunks to the wrong side of the brown square. Cut out the shapes on the drawn lines. Remove the paper backing.

5. Refer to the quilt assembly diagram on page 88 and the photo on page 84 to arrange three of the still-pinned, large whole trees on the background first. Position a tree trunk under the lower section of each tree. Position the three small trees on the mountain as desired. Once you are satisfied with the position of the trees, remove all of the pinned, large tree pieces except the tree trunk, keeping the pieces from each tree together. Fuse the trunks and the small trees in place, following the manufacturer's instructions.

6. Unpin and center the widest section of each of the three large trees in place over the trunk,

using the fold line as a guide; pin in place. Use a walking or even-feed foot to stitch ¼" from the sides and bottom of each piece.

7. Stitch the three remaining pieces of each tree in place in the same manner, working from the widest to the narrowest. Center each piece over the previous piece, using the folds as a guide. Overlap the pieces slightly to cover the upper edge of the previous piece. Stitch around all sides of the narrowest piece.

8. Arrange the pieces of the remaining tree in order, including the trunk. Use your rotary cutter and ruler to cut the tree in half vertically, using the cutting lines as a guide.

9. Refer to the quilt assembly diagram to position the right half of the tree along the left side of the background piece. Fuse the trunk in place and then stitch the tree sections to the background in the same manner as the whole trees. Set aside the left section of the tree.

Finishing

1. Measure the quilt top for borders as instructed in "Step 8: Add the Borders" on page 13. Cut the 5"-wide inner border strips to the required length and stitch them to the quilt sides through all of the layers. Press toward the borders. Position the left tree half on the right border aligning the straight edge with the edge of the strip. Fuse the trunk in place and then stitch the shapes in place in the same manner as the previous trees. Cut and piece the 1¾"-wide inner border strips to the required length and stitch them to the top and bottom edges of the quilt top. Piece and cut the outer border strips and stitch them to the quilt top in the same manner.

2. Insert additional decorative quilting inside each shape of the large trees as desired. Outline quilt around the small trees and the tree trunks.

3. Bind the quilt edges.

4. Hand stitch the beads to the trees as desired.

5. Add a hanging sleeve and label.

Quilt Assembly Diagram

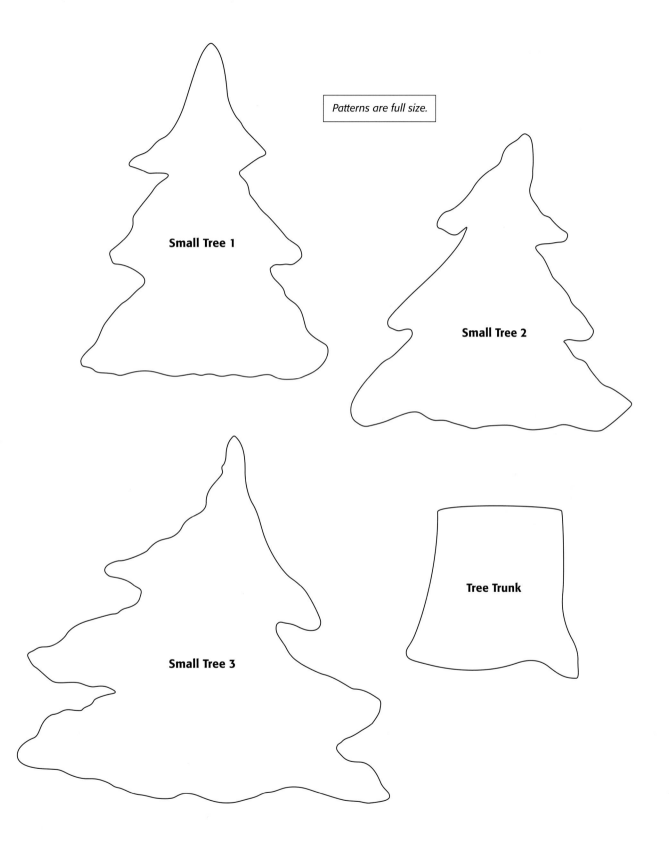

Patterns are full size.

Small Tree 1

Small Tree 2

Small Tree 3

Tree Trunk

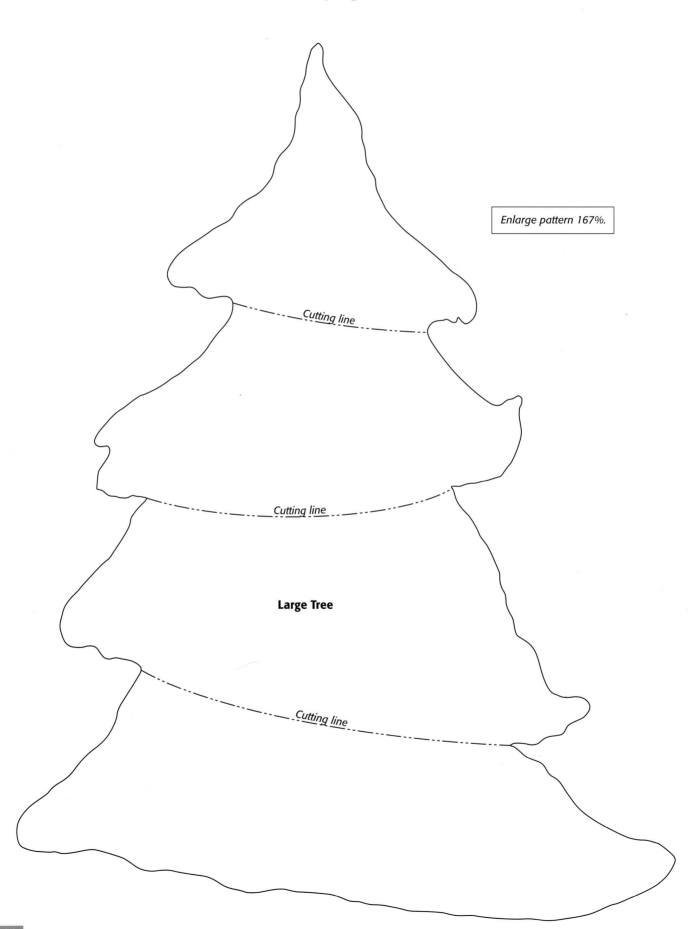

Enlarge pattern 167%.

Cutting line

Cutting line

Large Tree

Cutting line

DANCING STARS

Finished Quilt Size: 45½" x 53"
Finished Block Size: 11½" x 17"

Pieced by Jayme Crow. Machine quilted by Sandy Sims, Heirloom Originals.

Twinkle, twinkle, dancing stars, adding dazzle from afar. Keep us warm and give us light, guide us through a wintry night.

—Joan and Jayme

Materials

Yardage is based on 42"-wide fabric.

- ❖ 1 fat quarter *each* of 6 coordinating bright color fabrics for sashing and stars
- ❖ 1¼ yards of multicolor wide-stripe fabric for block backgrounds
- ❖ 1 yard of fabric for border
- ❖ 3 yards of fabric for backing
- ❖ ½ yard of fabric for binding
- ❖ 53" x 60" piece of batting
- ❖ 6 buttons, ½" diameter (optional)
- ❖ Air-soluble marker
- ❖ Freezer paper
- ❖ Spray starch

Cutting

All measurements include ¼"-wide seam allowances.

From *each* fat quarter, cut:
1 strip, 4½" x 12", along the short edge

From the multicolor stripe, cut:
6 rectangles, 12½" x 18"

From the border fabric, cut:
5 strips, 6" x 42"

From the backing fabric, cut:
2 pieces, 30" x 53"

From the binding fabric, cut:
6 strips, 2¼" x 42"

Cutting the Stars

1. Enlarge star patterns A and B on page 95 by the percentage indicated. Trace the enlarged stars and star patterns C and D on page 94 onto freezer paper and cut them out.
2. Referring to the diagram below, use the templates to cut one each of stars A, B, C, and D from the remainder of each of the six fat quarters.

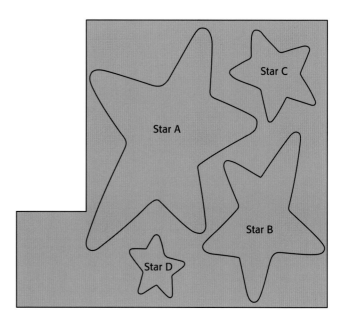

Making the Blocks

1. Iron the star shapes and block background rectangles, applying spray starch for stability while sewing. Fold the background rectangles in half vertically and horizontally and lightly press the folds to mark the centers.
2. Using the air-soluble marker, mark the cutting line on each star.

3. Select a star B shape for each star A shape and a star D shape for each star C shape.

4. To make the large star units, position a star B over each star A, right sides up, aligning the cutting lines; pin in place. Stitch around each star B, ¼" from the raw edge. Cut away the star A fabric behind the star B shape, leaving a ¼" seam allowance.

5. Cut each star unit on the marked cutting line, using a rotary cutter and ruler.

6. Select a different upper star portion for each lower star portion. When you are satisfied with all of the arrangements, stitch the new stars together. Press the seams open.

7. To make the small star units, position a star D over each star C, aligning the cutting lines; pin in place. Stitch around each star D, ¼" from the raw edge. Cut away the star C fabric behind the star D shape, leaving a ¼" seam allowance. Repeat steps 5 and 6 to complete the small star units.

8. Position a small star unit on each large star unit as desired; pin in place. Experiment with tilting the stars for a different effect. Stitch ¼"

from the raw edges of each star C. Cut away the star fabric behind the small star unit, leaving a ¼" seam allowance. Press the units from the wrong side.

9. Center a star unit on each background rectangle, using the fold lines as a guide; pin in place. Stitch around each star A, ¼" from the raw edges. Do not cut away the background fabric behind the star.

10. Press each block. Square up each block to 12" x 17½".

Assembling the Quilt Top

1. Refer to the quilt assembly diagram on page 94 to arrange the blocks and the 4½" x 12" sashing strips into three vertical rows of two blocks and two sashing strips each. Stitch the pieces in each row together. Press the seams in opposite directions from row to row. Stitch the rows together.

2. Measure the quilt top for borders as instructed in "Step 8: Add the Borders" on page 13. Piece and cut the side borders to the required length and stitch them to the sides of the quilt top. Repeat for the top and bottom borders.

Finishing

Refer to "Finishing Your Quilt" on pages 15–17.

1. Layer the quilt top with backing and batting; baste.
2. Beginning with the blocks in the center of the quilt, quilt around each star unit, working from the smallest star toward the largest. Echo quilt the star shape in the background. Repeat the star motif to quilt the border.
3. Bind the quilt edges.
4. Hand stitch a button to the center of each star unit, if desired.
5. Add a hanging sleeve and label.

Quilt Assembly Diagram

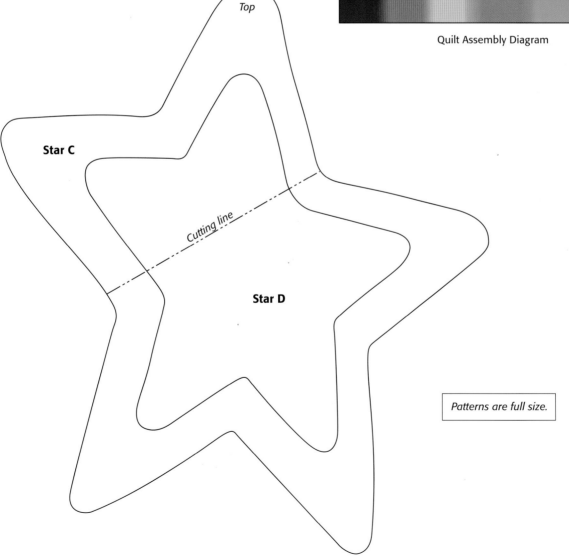

Patterns are full size.

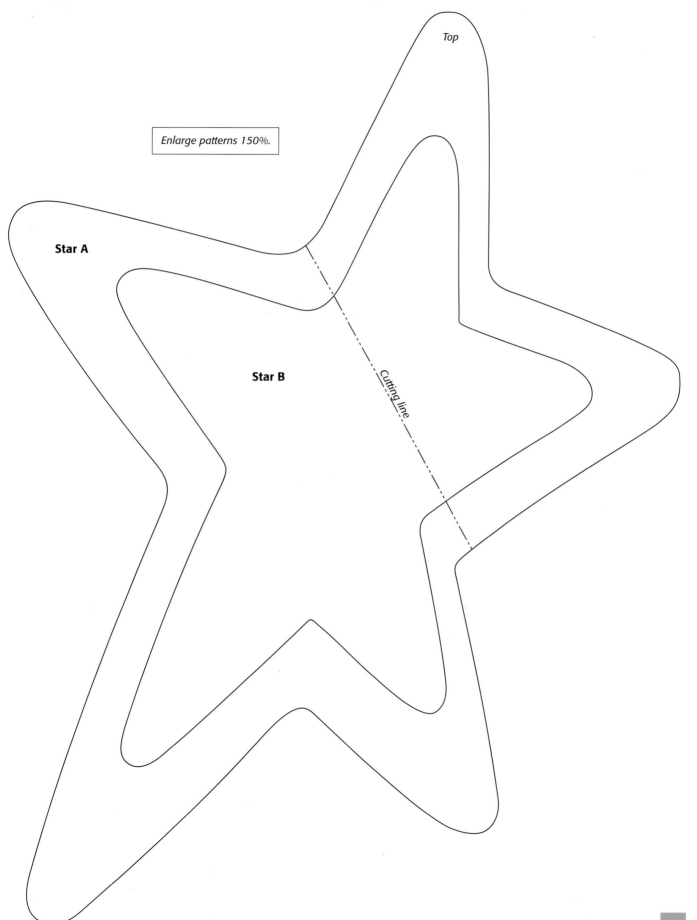

Top

Enlarge patterns 150%.

Star A

Star B

Cutting line

Jayme Crow

Jayme grew up in Walla Walla, Washington, and now lives in Kennewick, Washington, with her husband, Jim. She has two grown daughters, Lindsay and Megan, who grew up creating with Mom. As a young girl, she discovered a love of fabric and began her sewing career. Her first project was a white eyelet apron that her grandmother helped her create from a Swedish apron pattern. The first sewing project she tackled alone was a tailored jacket she made from a Vogue pattern. She treasures the now-tattered eyelet apron and still has the jacket hanging in the back of her closet. At age 19, while living in Germany, she started an eclectic collection of fabric and laces she found in her travels around Europe.

Jayme's passion for quilting has grown out of a love for combining color, design, and fabrics. She enjoys teaching and learning from others to expand her knowledge of textile and design. She has many projects going at once and draws from things around her to inspire new ideas. While indulging in her delight for gardening, she often dreams up new ideas to try in the design studio.

Joan Segna

Joan grew up in San Bernardino, California, and now lives in Richland, Washington, with her husband, Don. Before moving to Richland, they spent 17 years as part of the NASA Manned Spacecraft Center community south of Houston, Texas—fun and exciting years for both of them. Now a part of the Tri-Cities community on the Columbia River, they both feel very much a part of this friendly Northwest desert community. They have three grown children, two daughters and a son, all interesting and creative in their own right.

Fabric has been a part of Joan's life for as long as she can remember, from her early days "picking out" the material for her mother to sew into dresses, to her own adventures sewing doll clothes and, eventually, that first gathered skirt. The broad experience she has gained from living in diverse regions of the United States influences Joan's choice of color and texture.

Joan has studied all aspects of fiber, including weaving, tailoring, and fiber art. She studied art and design in college and studied oil painting for six years. Quilting is the perfect blend of her love of art, design, color, and fabric. Her oil paintings and pencil drawings have been displayed in several juried shows.